Encinitas, Ca

LOADED WORDS

Freeing 12 Hard Bible Words from Their Baggage

Leann Luchinger
Heather Choate Davis

Dear Madeleine & Frank — helping push ... me in love ... work

ICKTANK
PRESS

Cover design by Lon Davis.

The Twelve Steps are reprinted with permission of Alcoholics Anonymous World Services, Inc. ("AAWS") Permission to reprint the Twelve Steps does not mean that AAWS has reviewed or approved the contents of this publication, or that AAWS necessarily agrees with the views expressed herein. A.A. is a program of recovery from alcoholism <u>only</u> - use of the Twelve Steps in connection with programs and activities which are patterned after A.A., but which address other problems, or in any other non-A.A. context, does not imply otherwise. Additionally, while A.A. is a spiritual program, A.A. is not a religious program. Thus, A.A. is not affiliated or allied with any sect, denomination, or specific religious belief.

The Next Christendom: The Coming of Global Christianity nu Jenkins (2011) 300w from pp.3, 21, 23, 25, 29, 32-33. By permission of Oxford University Press, USA (www.oup.com).

Dedicated to the wise and thoughtful theologians
who've helped us along the way:
Father Mussie Berhe,
Dr. James Bachman,
Dr. Mark Brighton,
Dr. David Loy,
Dr. Korey Maas,
Dr. Michael Middendorf,
and Dr. Steven Mueller.

4

PREFACE

The most important thing about this book is that it gives us all—yet again—clear evidence of God at work in the lives of His people, using them in new and unexpected ways. Leann Luchinger and Heather Choate Davis started the MA Theology program at Concordia University in Irvine, CA at the same time. Each had been exposed to the church in their youths, but neither had become devout believers until their children entered Lutheran elementary schools—same time, same journey, different cities. They were both lifelong learners and self-proclaimed "nerds." They each trusted wholly and blindly (and often times foolishly) that by the end of the program God would make it clear what they were to do with their theological training.

For two years, they wrote and dialogued and pelted the professors with questions, each earning top marks with wildly different learning styles. After four hours of night classes, they would continue their dialectics in their cars over speaker phone. They not only sought to understand but to tease out applications for all they were learning.

The idea they returned to again and again was loaded words. Because every time a key faith term was explained in its original context or language they noticed that it felt like an entirely different animal than the word most heard back in the pews—and certainly what most heard in the culture. As experts in communications—and with keen ears for the nuances of language—they found themselves saying each week, "If people really understood what these words meant they wouldn't have such a hard time believing." Their shorthand became so crisp that after an elaborate theological concept was reviewed in class they would catch each other's eye across the room, lift up their hands emphatically, and say, "loaded words!"

The day after Leann made her thesis presentation to the CUI Theology Department, Heather was there. She stayed over at the Luchinger house nearby—a habit they'd developed to spare Heather the drive back to L.A. and allow their conversations to extend from breakfast till bedtime. Leann's husband, who had been observing their feverish discourses throughout the program, went to his office, came back to the table and fanned out five $100 Hyatt gift cards. "This is your seed money. Go somewhere and start your think tank." By the end of the day Heather and Leann had named their new company icktank. They already knew what their first project would be. "Two by two they were sent," Scripture tells us. May His hand be evident in all you encounter in these pages.

TABLE OF CONTENTS

"Therefore a scribe who has been trained for the kingdom of heaven is like the master of a household who brings out of his treasure what is new and what is old" (Matthew 13:52).

Chapter 1

WORD

No matter who you are or what you believe, you'll likely agree that we all have at least one thing in common: we are drowning in words. We wake up to them on our radios and play lists. We are bombarded with them in blogs, newscasts, billboards, emails, paperwork, texts and tweets. And when we think we can't process another phrase, we collapse in front of our favorite shows—smart phone in hand—where we are soothed with dialogue and the loud promises of pitchmen. A 2009 study (which in digital terms is "the good old days") revealed that the average American encounters 34 gigabytes of content and 100,000 words of information in a single day.[1]

In Dr. Seuss's 1940 book Horton Hatches an Egg the faithful elephant exclaims, "I meant what I said and I said what I meant." This line was once synonymous with virtue and integrity, but notice what's missing in the claim: truth. A person can say what they mean and mean what they say but what they mean and say—and often repeat to anyone who will listen—may or may not be true. The more we use words, the more they tend to lose their original meaning.

This has created a real problem for those who love the Gospel. Because we have tossed the words of Scripture around so carelessly in the culture—sometimes innocently, sometimes not— many people who've never stepped inside a church now feel they know everything they need to know about Christianity: "thanks, but no thanks." This negative bias has been formed, in no small part, by our own words. Words that have not been used thoughtfully. Words we simply didn't understand well enough to explain. Words we have tweaked from the original meaning to better suit our own comfort or agenda or, perhaps, in a misguided pursuit of cultural relevance.

Playing fast and loose with language is hardly an offense unique to Christians. In the modern era—where our educational system has all but severed ties with the Latin, Greek, and Hebrew roots that might keep us moored—words can now mean whatever we want them to mean. The Oxford English Dictionary made that clear when it voted, in 2013, to include the wholly opposite meaning for the word "literally" as a now-acceptable definition simply because so many people had taken to using it that way. The thinking goes, if people just don't seem to be able to understand how to use "literally" to mean, "exact, actual, in fact," well, then, we should just allow for this new meaning.[2]

This evolving paradigm of language has grave consequences when it comes to Scripture. What happens when people no longer understand the meaning of, for example, "sin." Does the church just adopt a lesser definition, one that is easier to swallow? Easier to dismiss? And how are we to understand the meaning of words when our information marketplace is peopled with commentators who no longer adhere to the fundamental journalistic tradition of fact-finding and fairness. Their words seem to be serving a new paradigm: if people like what you're saying, keep saying it. Popularity, not truth, is the benchmark of our communications era.

When the world was primarily non-literate, the spoken word was held to a much higher standard. Sincerity and personal integrity in one's speech were essential. A spoken oath was considered inviolable in commercial, judicial, and civic affairs. This applied equally to everyday speech, where the use of words that were foolish, disingenuous, malicious, blasphemous, or skewed to the users advantage were all considered an affront. This level of verbal integrity stayed with us for a very long time. The term "gentlemen's agreement" is credited in the OED to P.D. Wodehouse in his 1929 story "Mr. Mulliner Speaking." By definition it is an agreement that is only binding as a matter of honor.

The saying "My word is my bond," comes from the 1923 Coat of Arms mounted on the wall of the London Stock Exchange. From the Latin *dictum meum pactum*, it defined the terms and conditions for an industry run without any exchange of documents or written contracts. Simply this: my word, my bond. This honor code approach to life is only possible in a society that sees a person's word as sacred.

This was how the Hebrews used the most common term for word, *dā·ḇār*. We see it in Genesis 11:1, "Now the whole earth had one language and the same *words*." We see it again in Genesis 15:1, "After these things *the word* of the Lord came to Abram in a vision…" This same word—*dā·ḇār*—is used when God spoke to Moses, giving him "the ten words." That's what they're called—literally: *the ten words.* In fact, nowhere in all of the original language of Scripture are they called *The Ten Commandments*, but that's how we've come to use them. This speaks volumes to the world, teaching that ours is a faith based on shoulds and shouldn'ts, when the triune God said no such thing.[3]

The most common term for "word" in Greek—the predominant language of the New Testament—is *logos*. The word was already in use in the culture just before Christ's birth. Philo of Alexandria, a faithful Jew and an Egyptian scholar, was already connecting the dots between the Wisdom tradition of Jewish theology and the Logos of Greek philosophy, referring to the Logos as the divine mediator in creation, revelation, and all God's dealings with men, as the active agent of God's outgoing power.[4] Some consider this moment, these connections—this *word*—as the gateway to the flashpoint in human history. *Logos*. John is the first one to use it as the God-given identity of Jesus Christ[5]—John, the Gospel writer who was given the final word in Scripture. "And the Word became flesh and dwelt among us, and we have seen his glory, glory as of the only Son from the Father, full of grace and truth" (John 1:14).

We are a long way off from this sacred understanding of what a "word" represents. According to the *Hyperlinked Life*, people of our information age believe there's less than a 50-50 chance that anything they read online is true.[6] Friends, co-workers, or those who have traditionally been considered "trustworthy" are no longer taken at their word. When the majority of Millennials—even practicing Christian Millennials—are now, according to the Barna Group, fact checking pastors' claims during the sermon, it seems fair to say that this means of grace, whether through distrust or inattention, is being compromised.

In the coming chapters we will look at words that, over time, in ways large and small, innocent and willful, we the church and we the culture have abused, and in doing so, loaded them down with so much social, cultural, and doctrinal baggage that they are hard-pressed to convey grace. We hope to look at these "loaded words" anew, to see and hear them the way Jesus intended, and in some small way, to restore them to their ordained standard as bearers of grace and truth.

WORD
UNLOADED

- We live in an era that is reliant on words, but our words are no longer reliable.

- Words that help communicate the Gospel must be stripped of spin and confusion and returned to their original understanding.

- The apostle John uses *logos*—Word—as the God-given identity of Jesus Christ.

Study Questions
WORD

1. Do you use email, Facebook, Twitter, text messaging, or other electronic communication tools? Do you listen to talk radio or television news? How many kinds of advertising messages are you exposed to in a day? How many words do you think you read or hear each day?

2. Can you think of a word that has changed in use and meaning? Is the original definition still used or has it been abandoned entirely? What are the consequences of this word's new definition?

3. On page 12 we read: "My word is my bond." What does this mean to you? Do you think it works anywhere in the culture today?

4. Can you imagine the NYSE being run as a "gentleman's agreement" today? What if all the traders were Christian—then would it work?

5. Considering question 3 above, READ John 1:1-5. We call Jesus Christ the *Word* of God. And we say the Holy Scriptures are the *Word* (Jesus) in words (the Bible). What do you think this means about God, Jesus, and the Bible?

Chapter 2

SIN

There is probably no religious word more divisive, more inflammatory, more offensive—or more essential—than *sin*. Many people today believe that it's a distinctly Christian word, a big, fat, finger-wagging word that The Church uses to shame people into behaving. Although some in the modern church do—sadly—use it in this way, the word *sin* does not belong to the Christian church. It belongs to, and has been used by, all people since the beginning of recorded time. Ancient people from all tribes and nations have shared a common understanding that all things come from God or the gods, and that sin puts them at odds with their source of life.[1] Early cultures, from Africa, to India, to South America, to the pluralistic Jewish, Roman, and pagan world into which Jesus entered, understood—not just intellectually, but viscerally—that sin was the central flaw in the human condition and that it put both individuals and communities at risk. And they sinned just as egregiously and insidiously as we do today.

In the 21st century, we've come to view sin in one of three ways: as a dusty relic of a high church era, as a private matter between ourselves and God, or as something someone else does that's much worse than what we do. But sin is neither obsolete, nor personal, nor relative. Sin was, is, and always will be, that little voice we all share that rises up in our psyche, our spirit, our gut any time we sense opposition to our desires, declaring war.

The biblical vocabulary of *sin* is rich and varied, echoing the historic preoccupation with the human condition. The original meanings range from singular acts of transgression to the sweeping downward spiral of an entire life. The root concepts in both the Hebrew and the Greek are similar. *Hāṭā,* the primary Hebrew root for sin, means to miss, to incur guilt, and to forfeit. *Hamartia*, the primary Greek root means to miss a mark or target, to disobey, or to fail to live up to expectations. The failure to respect the full rights and interests of others and the disruption of interpersonal relationships as a consequence are **always** a factor. [2]

Included, also, in the family of sin lexicon are two word forms that refer specifically to the "sin offering." This notion seems barbaric to modern ears, but was utterly commonplace and wholly understood in both

Hebrew and ancient pagan cultures. A sacrifice of something valued—often involving burning or bleeding, coupled with repentance—was understood to be necessary to "get right" or restore their broken relationships with God (or the gods) and neighbor. How, you might ask, does burning and bleeding help repair relations with friends and family? It doesn't. The act of seeking reconciliation with one's neighbor does that, but the ritual brings visible, communal closure. The community recognizes that the final word is God's, that God alone knows what transpired between conflicted or estranged parties, that God alone can judge the human heart. In the earliest years of the formation of His people, He established these sacrifices to silence the agitators and bring those who strayed back into the fold. It was universally accepted that any gesture that was deemed good enough for God was deemed good enough for everyone else. Case closed. And so from those symbolic offerings, slates were wiped clean.

Lastly, there are metaphoric words for sin such as the Hebrew *sûr,* the spirit of which is captured in this well-known Isaiah passage, "All we like sheep have gone astray; we have turned—every one—to his own way..." (53:6). The nuance here emphasizes vainly wandering as a result of one's pretended autonomy.[3] This same word can also indicate the idea of sliding down the road to ruin—or backsliding—a common term in today's Recovery movement. Notice how our modern notion of

the "slippery slope" traces back to the God-given wisdom
of the Jews.

This search for Divine wisdom forever leads us
back to the Garden. Here is where the concept of sin is
first introduced and where our greatest misconceptions
about sin are rooted. First off, the word *sin* is never
actually used in the story of Adam and Eve and the eating
of the forbidden fruit—not in the Hebrew, or the Greek,
or the Latin, or any modern scholarly translation. There
are two assumptions that tend to cling to this story, one
true, one false. The true one is that this act of
disobedience is the *first act of sin.* This is correct.
Because it was the first time that little voice rose up in a
human being "declaring war" on the one restriction he
had been given: "You may surely eat of every tree of the
garden, but of the tree of the knowledge of good and evil
you shall not eat…" (Genesis 2:16-17).

The second very common but false assumption, is
that this moment—which is often referred to as The
Fall—is about sex. It isn't. But before we share a few
thoughts on how this misconception likely arose, it's
important to understand the way in which sex was viewed
in the Greco-Roman world, particularly in the context of
sin. The Greek elite placed a high premium on self-
restraint. Gluttony, drunkenness, anger, and cruelty were
considered the most egregious offenses, while sex—
although thought to be a dangerous and draining

distraction, especially for males—was a relatively "soft" sin.

So how did this sin/sex connection become so closely aligned with Christianity? It likely began due to several lines of thinking developed by important theologians in the early church who attempted to connect the dots from Genesis 3 to the practical realities of Paul's mysterious assertion in Romans 5:12: "Therefore, just as sin came into the world through one man, and death through sin, and so death *spread* to all men because all sinned—" (*emphasis ours*). St. Augustine, one of the most prolific writers of the early church—and a man who spent the better part of his teens and 20s having *a lot* of sex—was the first to connect "the transmission of original sin…with the pleasure of sexual intercourse."[4] Approaching this theological question like a scientist, he envisioned that sin set off in the first man and woman a disordered state of sexual desire that was wholly contrary to the conscious control of the mind and will, qualities which were God's gifts to those whom he entrusted with "dominion" over His creation.[5] It was through this loss of control, Augustine theorized, that sin was inherited.

As foolish as that might sound today, we need to be mindful that every narrative is shaped through the course of history, often accumulating unwanted or inaccurate baggage along the way. Those inclined to dismiss Augustine and his ilk outright for this thinking might want to consider what else we'd be losing. Here, one of the most sensual and soul-searing verses ever written about the path from resistance to faith:

> Late have I loved you, O Beauty ever ancient, ever new,
> Late have I loved you! You were within me, but I was outside,
> and it was there that I searched for you.
> In my unloveliness I plunged into the lovely things
> which you created.
> You were with me, but I was not with you.
> Created things kept me from you;
> yet if they had not been in you they would have not been at all. You called, you shouted, and you broke through my deafness. You flashed, you shone, and you dispelled my blindness.
> You breathed your fragrance on me; I drew in breath and now I pant for you. I have tasted you, now I hunger and thirst for more. You touched me, and I burned for your peace.
> —*The Confessions,* St. Augustine

Another sin/sex thread, then, was the delicate balancing act of understanding how God's command to "be fruitful and multiply" could be tied to something "sinful." Many came to defend the position that sex that was "procreative" was pleasing to God, but sex for the sheer pleasure of it was not. As for the current understanding of the seminal Romans 5:12 passage, most modern theologians across the denominational spectrum interpret it to mean something more like this: because we are human, like Adam, the reflex towards disobedience is now, since the Fall, in our nature; just as he rebelled, so too, we will rebel against God, leading us to death.

But why? This is another premise that is bewildering to modern ears—the relationship between sin and death. How did these ideas come to be paired? This sin/death connection is, again, a notion that has become linked to Christianity, but in fact, was established long before Jesus came on the scene. First off, despite Hollywood depictions of Roman excess, most throughout the empire lived a meager existence and were convinced that their poverty came as a result of a divine curse.[6] A curse was viewed as a punishment for wrongdoing and, since provisions such as rain and good crops were needed by all, sinners were considered deviants who jeopardized everyone's shot at, not only a good life but, any life at all.[7] Many of these were uneducated pagans who worshipped a variety of gods—ancestral, civic, Eastern, etc. Their sin-leads-to-death worldview came about without any exposure to the Law of Moses, and long before the mystery of the One who would pay the price for sin "once for all" (Romans 6:10).

Meanwhile, on the other side of the Mediterranean—and with no evident exposure to the teaching of the Torah—the highly-educated, utterly truth-seeking philosophers of Greece were drawing the same conclusion. In a Platonic dialogue known as *Gorgias*, Socrates speaks of a man who has done evil. He compares him to "a person who is afflicted with the worst of diseases and yet contrives not to pay the penalty to the physician for his sins against his constitution, and will not be cured, because, like a child, he is afraid of the pain of being burned or cut." He goes on to make the case that, so great is the torture of unpunished sin that a wise man, knowing he has acted unjustly or has done harm to another will "run to the judge, as he would to the physician, in order that the disease of injustice may not be rendered chronic and become the incurable cancer of the soul." He concludes that there is a punishment worse than death, which is to remain alive and be "immortal in his wickedness."[8]

Five hundred years before sin=death became Scripture, these brilliant Greek thinkers were already, unwittingly, setting the stage for the "sin offering" made flesh, and the radical gift of salvation in Christ, the one who "has suffered for us and that for His sake our sin is forgiven and righteousness and eternal life are given to us."[9]

Today, we feel we are i-years away from this sort of thinking. We tossed the word *sin* out with the sexual revolution, reducing it, much as Augustine had done, to a single act—sex—and then deciding, as a culture, we had somehow transcended the need for sexual restrictions. So, too, we try to toss the word *death* out with hair color, plastic surgery, medication, technology, second marriages, second families—deluding ourselves into thinking we are winning the battle. And yet, here we are, still in the flesh, still resistant, still demanding, still self-absorbed, and increasingly anxious, crying out in the night, "Who will deliver me from this body of death?" (Romans 7:24).

We have forgotten how to name our suffering, which only adds to the pain and the shame of our brokenness. The result, as C. S. Lewis explains in *The Problem of Pain*, is that "Christianity now has to preach the diagnosis—in itself very bad news—before it can win a hearing for the cure." Yet, even the church has minimized its discussion of *sin*, finding love and joy and hope and good works an easier sell. No doubt. But sin is where the rubber meets the road. Original sin, as Philip Melanchthon instructs, is far less about our disordered desires and far more about "the more serious defects of human nature like being ignorant of God, despising God, lacking fear and confidence in God, hating the judgment of God, fleeing this judging God, being angry with God, despairing of His grace, and placing confidence in temporal things."[10]   Unless we can come to an understanding of what the big picture of sin really is, whom it hurts, and how we might be free of its horrible burden, going to church has no more meaning than going to a company picnic. And steering clear of the hard truth of sin is just another step down the slippery slope.

Modern tales such as Shirley Jackson's *The Lottery* and the madly popular *Hunger Games* series resonate because of our primal understanding that a price must be paid for our secret little sins. In these stories, a new "sacrificial lamb" is chosen each year; as with Christ, it is always an innocent. Clearly *The Hunger Games*—much like the gladiator matches of Rome—are as much spectacle as expiation, but still, they offer the catharsis of casting our burden of guilt upon another. What they don't do is help us recognize our own sinfulness, and therefore can only illuminate, titillate, but never heal.

To help with that personal recognition we offer a new/old way to think about sin. *Homo Incurvatus in Se.* Man Turned in on Himself. This is one of those early threads that has been pulled through the narrative of the faith and somehow lost along the way. The idea had first been put forth in its simplest form by Augustine (yes, him again). He gave us an image of *sin* as incurvature, as man *curved down* towards his base roots and away from his divine birthright, chest held high, arms outstretched to the heavens. A thousand years later, Martin Luther grabbed hold of this thread and developed it into a full-blown theological understanding of sin: man turned in on himself, on his own desires, when what he was meant to be and do is turn outward, loving and serving others.[11] What?? *But what about me? What about my needs* that little voice cries out, foot stomping. (Are you starting to recognize the voice of sin?) Ok, here's an image to go with it: think Gollum, the pitiful, enslaved creature from J.R.R. Tolkien's *Lord of the Rings*, protecting his "precious."

Not familiar with Gollum? Try this. Picture a body curved inward—in the fetal position, for example. The shape of the curve does two things: 1) it protects and defends the thing it is turned in on, guarding it and the right to have it to oneself, preferably in the secret shadow of the curve, and 2) its curved form creates a barrier between the heart's desire and the things it wants to keep at bay: judgment, change, help, love, God. Even if we take God out of the conversation, the image maintains its potency: when man is turned in on his own desires, the world—despite man's best efforts to the contrary—becomes smaller and darker. Without the impetus or wherewithal to reverse his course, his condition gets progressively worse. Without access to any power greater than himself—and with the sudden realization that he is, in fact, only human—he becomes trapped in the "hamster wheel" of his own thoughts and enslaved by his own feelings and desires.[12]

Sound familiar? It should. Because we are all this way, the faithful and the unfaithful, the wise and the lowly, the flawed and those who pretend to be otherwise.

This is what unites us. That, and our capacity to love—
just that, just those. Without this realization, we "break
up the race of mankind into a multitude of isolated atoms,
touching, but not really connected with, one another,
instead of contemplating it as one great organic whole."[13]
Stripped of relationships, reduced to little more than
bytes of information, hertz of productivity, decimal
points of worth, our lives lose all meaning. We become
detached from the great narrative of mankind, and fall
into despair.

Still, when we are in this state it seems all but
impossible to think about someone else and their needs,
their suffering. This is what grace is for, to help us do that
which we cannot possibly do on our own; turn back to
God, turn out to others. Out, not in. This is the direction
in which we must turn, not only for the sake of our
neighbors but, ironically, for the realization of our highest
and best selves. This is the pay-off that man fails to see in
his "turned away" state. He hears the call to love
neighbor and instinctively flees when in truth, this path of
loving others *is* the very same path of becoming one's
highest and best. It is our own personal land of milk and
honey, where each gift will be fully utilized, each divot
patched up, and the fissures of our broken hearts slowly
mended until, on the last day, we are lifted up and made
whole for eternity.[14]

No pain, no gain. This is a secular understanding
of the same fundamental truth of the teaching of sin: no

honesty, no forgiveness. No repentance, no grace. Why, then, if we can so readily embrace the clever, worldly ideal, is it so hard to accept the foundational spiritual truth of our God-given lives? As you are now at the end of the chapter on Sin, you already know the answer.

SIN
UNLOADED

- Sin is our willful, human desire to be our own God.

- Sin puts both individuals and communities at risk.

- When we are turned in on ourselves, we are trapped in a state of sin.

- Sin always leads in the opposite direction of that which is life-giving.

Study Questions
SIN

1. What do you think of when you hear the word sin? Do you think of "sin" as an act or a state of being? What do you think people outside the church think of when they hear the word sin?

2. On page 18 we read: The failure to _____ the full rights and interests of _____ and the disruption of _____ as a consequence are always a factor. READ John 13:34-35. How do you think this Scripture passage and the preceding statement relate?

3. The opening pages give us some important explanations of how sin was understood by our biblical ancestors. What are some of the explanations or definitions you see? How does this inform your understanding of sin?

4. On page 20 we read that Adam and Eve in the Garden of Eden committed the first sin. What was this sin?

5. According to the explanations on pages 23-24, how did the sin/death connection get established? Who made these early connections?

6. After reading about *Homo Incurvatus in Se* on pages 26-27, can you think of any modern images of "man turned in on himself?"

7. Considering question 6 above, READ Matthew 22:36-40. Can you be turned in and love God and neighbor at the same time?

Chapter 3

REPENT

If you're not part of any sort of faith community, your primary exposure to the word "repent" is likely on the signs displayed by feverish "Christians" at public protests or special events. *Repent Sinner! Repent or Go to Hell!* Thoughtful believers recognize that this is not the most user-friendly way to talk about God, but the people who wield those signs insist that they are called to speak out. Unfortunately, these contentious signs almost always take words from Scripture—*repent* being chief among them—and twist and spin and reduce and shout them in ways that profoundly misrepresent the enduring truth of God.

The first, and perhaps, greatest error in the loud and threatening use of the word *repent* in the public square is that it makes use of "insider language" to speak outside to the culture. With very few exceptions, in

Scripture the word *repent* is used to speak to those who
already view their lives in the context of God. It is
language for people who have been taught the full
meaning of the word and are now being reminded by the
prophets, by Christ, by the Apostles, over centuries of
gatherings across the Holy Land, that the humble
recognition and confession of the ways in which we fall
short each day is an essential part of the journey. The
critical detail is this: always, in that same gathered crowd,
just along the fringes, both then and now, there are a few
stirred souls who approach uncertainly, leaning in, the
people in whom God is in the process of awakening faith
and the impulse to turn to Him. It is with these people in
mind that God tells us through Paul, "The Lord's servant
must not be quarrelsome but kind to everyone, able to
teach, patiently enduring evil, correcting his opponents
with gentleness. God may perhaps grant them repentance
leading to a knowledge of the truth" (2 Timothy 2:24-26).

The second fault of the sign-waver approach is the
pairing of the word "repent" with the word "Hell." Now,
in terms of a sound bite it packs a lot of punch, but it is,
again, scripturally inaccurate. Because nowhere in all of
the Bible will you find a single sentence in which both
the word *repent* and the word *Hell* appear. The story of
God's saving work is simply never presented in that
highly reductive form. The closest paraphrase would be
found in Luke 13:3, "Unless you repent, you will all
likewise perish."

This passage from Luke is also found frequently on the emphatic banners in the public sphere. What the signs fail to say is what prompts Jesus to speak these words in the first place. The scene looked something like this: Pontius Pilate, a high-ranking Roman authority, had just ordered the execution of some of God's people, who were worshipping in the Temple of Jerusalem. The committing of a violent act in a sacred place is considered a particularly heinous act—even now. For many, the fact that these worshippers had been slaughtered—in the temple no less—was incontrovertible evidence that they must have committed a great, albeit secret, sin.[1] In other words, their massacre was somehow deserved.

The question, "Do you think that these Galileans were worse sinners than all the other Galileans, because they suffered in this way?" (Luke 13:2), reveals that Jesus sees right through them. The crowd was seeking reassurance that the slain were somehow "other" than themselves, but Jesus offered, instead, a call to examine their own hearts. It was as if he told the 21st-century protesters to flip their signs around and wave them in their own faces. "No, I tell you; but unless you repent, you will all likewise perish." This is just one of the many times in which Jesus turns the whole paradigm of lesser or greater sins—and lesser or greater judgment—on its head. All fall short. All are in need of repentance. Always.

A final concern about the homemade-sign approach is the complete lack of factual oversight in even the simplest phrases. Case in point: a newspaper photograph of a protester with a sign that incorrectly cites the aforementioned verse from Luke 13:3 as Isaiah 55:6. What the Old Testament prophet Isaiah actually said in this verse is, "Seek the Lord while he may be found, call upon him while he is near." Ironically, *this* is the sort of message much better suited for the public square.

Now that we're clear on how *repent* is not to be used, let's look more closely at how we *are* intended to hear, understand, and apply it. In Hebrew, the first language of Scripture, there are two words that are translated as *repent*: one is *nāham* and the other is *šûḇh*. The latter includes a rich variety of nuances on the theme of *turning back* including *to turn to, to be returned, to restore, to be recovered, to be brought back, to restore relationship, to bring home, and to consider.*[2]

Because Hebrew is the language of Abraham, Isaac, and Jacob, the covenantal relationship with God undergirds all these words. *Returning*, then—one of the most common meanings—never indicates a secular context, i.e., "Let's return next week to that oasis where they had the great dates and honey." The deep, personal, rock bottom tone expressed by the prophet Joel is one of the purest representations of how *repent* is used: "'Yet even now,' declares the Lord, '*return to me* with all your heart, with fasting, with weeping, and with mourning'"

(Joel 2:12). Notice that repentance is not a judgment, but an invitation initiated by God with an inherent and assured promise of forgiveness.

The concept of repentance is wholly visible in every culture in the world, regardless of religion or lack thereof. Our simplest model is in the home where daily children are taught that they need to say, "I'm sorry." Picture the pouting, quivering, mouth of a 3-year old who has gone too far. Maybe they didn't want to share a toy and ended up smacking their playmate with it. Maybe they called their brother "stupid" or refused to listen to a parent's reminder not to interrupt. To an outside observer, the child's behavior is almost comical—the tightly crossed arms, the fat, salt tears, the stomping off to the room (or the time-out chair) as they hear those timeless words, "And don't *come back* until you're ready to say you're sorry." Inside the child there is a painful surge of new awareness. The realization that there is right and wrong, they can't do or say whatever they feel like, and there is an expectation of them to recognize this and "come clean."

This human cycle of I love you/But you need to say I'm sorry/I will forgive you/And all will be well again is an echo of what the Bible teaches about the cycle of grace, repentance, forgiveness, and reconciliation. Grace is a gift from God. *We* don't decide to love Him— He is always the initiator—but we choose whether or not to turn back to Him, to finally swallow our pride, accept the fact He is real, and, with remorse in our hearts, return home. When we do, God responds with another gift: forgiveness. As Philip Melanchthon reminds us, "a human being, particularly in the terrors of sin, cannot be sure of the will of God (namely, that he ceases to be angry) without a sure Word of God."[3] And when we know that we are forgiven, we can then use this same model in our interactions with other people, as we begin to reorient our lives from an inward to an outward turn.

This same "turning" root *šûḇh* underlies one of the common Greek words for repent: *epistrephō*.[4] One example of this word comes to us from Matthew 13:15, "For this people's heart has grown dull, and with their ears they can barely hear, and their eyes they have closed, lest they should see with their eyes and hear with their ears and understand with their heart and *turn*, and I would heal them." This healing of that which is broken is the end game: repentance is just the first (difficult, necessary, humbling) step. We see this model used in the culture with near-miraculous results in Bill W.'s 12-step model of recovery, originally created for Alcoholics Anonymous:

1. We admitted we were powerless over alcohol—that our lives had become unmanageable.
2. Came to believe that a Power greater than ourselves could restore us to sanity.

3. Made a decision to turn our will and our lives over to the care of God *as we understood Him*.
4. Made a searching and fearless moral inventory of ourselves.
5. Admitted to God, to ourselves, and to another human being the exact nature of our wrongs.
6. Were entirely ready to have God remove all these defects of character.
7. Humbly asked Him to remove our shortcomings.
8. Made a list of all persons we had harmed, and became willing to make amends to them all.
9. Made direct amends to such people wherever possible, except when to do so would injure them or others.
10. Continued to take personal inventory and when we were wrong promptly admitted it.
11. Sought through prayer and meditation to improve our conscious contact with God, *as we understood Him*, praying only for knowledge of His will for us and the power to carry that out.
12. Having had a spiritual awakening as the result of these Steps, we tried to carry this message to alcoholics, and to practice these principles in all our affairs. [5]

The 12 Steps are considered "spiritual principles," used by over 200 self-help organizations, which include millions of members gathered in small groups around the

world. Together they work on their "recovery," a key
meaning of the Hebrew word for *repent*. They do not
attempt to recover alone, but with the help of God and
others on a similar path. These recovery groups are most
often referred to as "fellowships." This same word—from
the Greek *koinonia*—means "communion," or a
community working in union with one another. It is the
same word that is used to describe the ideal functioning
of the Body of Christ.

The Recovery movement's model of
repentance—which has been intentionally implemented
apart from any specific church or religion—reminds us
that God is working at all times, in all ways, both in His
Church and in the world, to bring blessing and healing to
all. These 12 steps may also serve to help many who are
not suffering from any named substance abuse—just
ordinary everyday sinfulness—grow in their
understanding of what real repentance looks like.

Barring sociopaths, there is not a human being on
the planet that does not feel the need to repent. The
Jewish faithful express it on Yom Kippur. Muslim
believers prescribe to the word *tawba*, which is Arabic
for "a retreat" or "a return." Hindus incorporate cleansing
baths with a penitent heart and knowledge of the sacred
texts. In 1951, an Indian spiritual master, Maher Baba,
who claimed to be the Avatar, or God in human form,
penned this Prayer of Repentance that begins, "We
repent, O God most merciful; for all our sins; for every

thought that was false or unjust or unclean; for every word spoken that ought not to have been spoken…"[6] an echo of many Christian liturgical confessions.

When the clock strikes midnight each December 31st, all the world over, with little thought of God or sin, people greet the new year with repentant hearts. A New Year's resolution is nothing if not the recognition that something in one's life is creating more harm, pain, or damage than it is health, joy, or blessing—that it is a behavior that leads one closer to death than to life—and as such we make our best effort at reversing it. Simply put, we know it's time for a change. When we set out to make those changes without God or others, things tend not to go so well. Paul, who was, arguably, second only to Jesus in knowing how to create an opening for the Word of God for those who live outside His love, observes, "For godly grief produces a *repentance* that leads to salvation without regret, whereas worldly grief produces death" (2 Corinthians 7:10). Surely this is what we see each year as January turns to February, and the high hopes that despairing souls had of healing themselves without the help of community have been dashed, leaving people more discouraged and defensive and hopeless than ever. It is to these that Peter offers this word of consolation: "Repent therefore, and turn to God, so that your sins may be blotted out, that times of refreshing may come from the presence of the Lord" (Acts 3:19-20).

Although biblical translation leads us to understand repentance as a "turning back," the recovery movement may help us even more with their understanding of repentance as "I can't." I can't do this anymore. I can't go on like this. I can't fix it on my own. I can't survive without a power greater than myself. This is the hole, according to *Mere Christianity*, that each man and woman finds themselves in at one point or another. "Fallen man is not simply an imperfect creature who needs improvement; he is a rebel who must lay down his arms."[7]

So it is that we fall on our knees in the dark on the path we were so certain about and cry out to some unnamed source of power, "*I can't.*" This SOS is the essence of Christian *repentance*, a word that will never judge you, never fail you, and always inspire the Living God to come alongside you, His Son gently lifting you up, and helping you find your way back home.

REPENT
UNLOADED

- Repent is a returning, recovering or restoring word.

- Repent is an invitation, *not* a judgment.

- Repentance is the path to forgiveness.

- To repent is a universal human need.

Study Questions
REPENT

1. When you hear the word *repent*, what comes to mind? How do you think someone outside of the Christian faith hears this word?

2. Who, as we read on pages 33-34, is the word *repent* intended to be directed toward? Why?

3. According to the authors, on page 34, where in the Bible do you find the words *repent* and *Hell* in the same sentence?

4. What are some of the biblical definitions for the word *repent* you read in the chapter.

5. Do you know people who are in some sort of 12-step program? Do you recognize the relationship between the 12 steps and a biblical understanding of repentance? Do they?

6. READ Joel 2:12-13. How does it make you feel when you read on page 37: Repentance is not a judgment, but an _____ initiated by _____ with an inherent and assured promise of _____?

Chapter 4

HELL

One of the most memorable bits of dialogue in the past decade of TV comedy involves the narcissistic anchorman, Tom Tucker, from the animated series *Family Guy*:

> TOM: "Can my wife, Stacey, get you anything?"
> STACEY: "Go to Hell, Tom."
> TOM: "Already there, hun."[1]

This brief exchange speaks volumes about our views of Hell—as both a place of punishment where those who mistreat people deserve to be banished, as well as a state of being that is incessantly tormenting. The deeper theological meanings of Hell are not much more complicated.

As all understanding of Scripture begins with the Hebrew, we will look first at the word *Shĕ'ōl*. In early Hebrew thought, *Sheol* was considered the abode of the dead: *all* dead. The destination was not tied to behavior or punishment but simply to the cessation of life. When, in Isaiah 14, it is prophesied that kings and leaders will join everyone else in *Sheol*, all the ordinary dead cry out, "You too have become as weak as we! You have become like us!" (v.10b). Here we are shown the hard truth that death is the great equalizer, that all men will have "maggots" for a bed, and "worms" for a covering. No distinction is made on moral grounds.[2]

The early Hebrew understanding is that death is the moment at which we become cut off from God. Consider Psalm 88:3-5:

> For my soul is full of troubles,
> And my life draws near to *Sheol*.
> I am counted among those who go
> down to the Pit;
> I am a man who has no strength,
> like one set loose among the dead, like the slain
> that lie in the grave,
> like those whom you remember no more
> for they are cut off from your hand.

But *Sheol* not only lies on the border of life in the beyond, it also penetrates the circle of the living on every side, through sickness, oppression, betrayal, powerlessness, imprisonment by enemies, and ultimately death. Whenever we lose our sense of connection to God—or even the possibility of it—we experience the foretaste of *Sheol*. Dying, we discover then, is more than just a bio-physical process. It is the terminal disintegration of the life-relationship with Yahweh. It is the desperation man experiences whenever he feels he's been left for scrap—literally, spiritually, metaphorically —in the wilderness.[3]

This sense of *Sheol* is well captured by the prosaic phrase, "my life is a living hell," in Shakespeare's *Tempest* zinger, "Hell is empty and all the devils are here," or, more optimistically, in Winston Churchill's, "When you're going through Hell, keep going." Hell is a universal reference point. It only becomes problematic for people when it leaves the metaphorical and becomes tethered to an omnipotent God serving as the bouncer for all eternity.

So who's responsible for that—Jesus? Nope. Once again we turn to the Greeks, the gold standard for clear and reasoned thinking about truth.

In the 7th and 8th century BCE, hundreds of years before the first Christian writings, Greek poets begin to use the word *hades*. In Homer's *Illiad*, for example, *hades* represented the "god of the underworld and the abode of the dead who lead a shadowy existence in it."[4] Hades soon became the Greek equivalent of *Sheol*—the world of the dead— but over time, as the Greek sense of justice became more finely tuned, a new "afterlife metric" began to emerge. Yes, perhaps *all* the dead go to *hades*, but surely the righteous will be rewarded there, eternally speaking. Once there was a two-tiered system of "parting gifts," it was only a matter of time before the destinations would become delineated.

As the centuries drew nearer to the birth of Christ, other sources—Jewish, Greek, Ethiopian—began to reflect a new paradigm of the afterlife, one in which the souls of the righteous go to heaven, while the souls of the unrighteous go to *hades*. The word—again, a stand-in for *Sheol*—appears only occasionally in the New Testament. To give you a sense of relative importance, the word "wine," is used more than four times as often. When we do see *hades* in the NT, it has three different meanings depending on context: 1) death, 2) the place of all the dead, and 3) the place of the wicked dead only.[5] If the point the Gospel was trying to make was that bad people go to Hell to burn in agony forever, the Scripture writers were exceedingly vague about it.

As for the two actual words that are most closely aligned with our notion of flames and never-ending damnation, they do *not* actually translate as Hell. The first, *abyss*, is actually an adjective which means "bottomless, unfathomable," but in the New Testament came to represent the prison for demons. It is used only nine times[6] in the New Testament, seven of them in the wildly visual apocalyptic book of Revelation. From this *abyss*, subterranean fire rises, a prince named Apollyon[7] rules, weird creatures emerge including the beast or Antichrist,[8] and Satan is bound and held there for a thousand years (Revelation 20:1-3). Some Christians emphasize and align these images with a biblical notion of Hell, but, again, the word that Scripture uses—*abyss* – does not, in any translation, mean hell. The other is a Greek term *tartarus or tartaroō* meaning "lower regions." This image was popular in classical literature of the day, and is used only once,[9] to refer to the destination of fallen angels.

Which brings us to *gehenna,* the **primary** Greek term used to represent *hell* in the New Testament. This is the word Jesus uses. In fact, all but one of the 12 occurrences of the word *gehenna* come from Jesus's own lips.[10] *Gehenna* is from the Aramaic word for the Hebrew phrase "the Valley of Hinnom." It was typically identified with a deep ravine that ran from beneath the western wall of the Old City of Jerusalem toward the south.[11] It was a place of trash fires and perpetually burning rubbish, where corpses and ashes were tossed and notorious evil was conducted—including, most heinously, infant sacrifice.[12]   For ancient listeners, *gehenna* was synonymous with the most sinister behavior the world had ever known. The word likely conveyed the same potent, shuddering horror as *Auschwitz* does for us today.

As Jesus began a ministry that aimed to flip the whole paradigm of human behavior on its head—the insiders are out, the poor are rich, the neighbor is more precious than self—Jesus uses *gehenna* as an extreme example of the consequences of self-centered, self-aggrandizing, self-deluding acts and attitudes that exclude, diminish or harm *other people* and the fabric of community. The very first time the word *gehenna* is used, Jesus is trying to steer people away from the easy-to-skirt notion of sin as big, bad deeds like murder—you know, the things that other people—really bad people—do.

> You have heard that it was said to those of old, 'You shall not murder; and whoever murders will be liable to judgment.' But I say to you that everyone who is angry with his brother will be liable to judgment; whoever insults his brother will be liable to the council; and whoever says, 'You fool!' will be liable to the hell (*gehenna*) of fire (Matthew 5:21-22).

Let's review. The first time Jesus uses His exclusive word for *hell* it is to correct people for thinking "it's no big deal to call someone an idiot." This is where He sets the bar, and recalibrates all our priorities. The next time He uses *gehenna*, it is to radically expand the Jewish teaching about adultery.

> You have heard that it was said, 'You
> shall not commit adultery.' But I say to
> you that everyone who looks at a woman
> with lustful intent has already committed
> adultery with her in his heart. If your
> right eye causes you to sin, tear it out
> and throw it away. For it is better that
> you lose one of your members than that
> your whole body be thrown into hell
> (*gehenna*). And if your right hand causes
> you to sin, cut it off and throw it away.
> For it is better that you lose one of your
> members than that your whole body go
> into hell (*gehenna*) (Matthew 5:27-30).

We were given a firsthand look at this Scripture in
1976, when Jimmy Carter confessed that he had
"committed adultery in his heart many times."[13] America
squirmed, but President Carter knew what Jesus meant.
Once we start eyeing that new woman at the office, that
new guy at the gym, that desire alone taints the promise
of love and fidelity that we have pledged to a spouse. We
come up with terms like "fantasy life" to allow ourselves
wiggle room, but Jesus said clearly, "who are you
kidding?" Why? Is it because daydreaming about sex is
such a big deal? Once again, this is the wrong question.
It's because hurting people is such a big deal—for them,
for you, and for all the innocents caught up in our wake.
And so He makes it clear: the way that you are behaving
is going to create in you a destiny so *hellacious*, so

gehenna-esque, you will not, without the grace of God, be able to right it.

We really are familiar with hell on earth, if not in our own lives then around the world, where global atrocities occur with soul-numbing frequency. But Hell after death, Hell as judgment, Hell that is inescapably real—really? Thoughtful Christian scholars who dedicate their lives to answering this question agree on a great deal. The Apostles Creed, for example, which celebrates the shared understanding that "Jesus descended into hell" and then rose again on the third day fulfilling the Scriptures. But they also disagree on a few things, and it is not likely they will come to consensus in this lifetime for one primary reason: none of us can ever know for certain what lies beyond until we get there. Maybe if Jesus had elaborated a little more—but He didn't. Maybe if Hell were really an essential part of His message He would have.

But, but…what about all those things people say about Hell as a fiery place of eternal damnation? Well, there is fire imagery, for example, in Matthew where Jesus refers to a "furnace of fire"—in other words, a place where things that do not have value or good purpose are thrown away and destroyed like the garbage thrown into *gehenna*. Jesus, as we read in Mark and Luke as well, uses the vernacular and imagery of the day to stir in the gathered masses a sense of urgency: Listen! Take heed.[14] Consider your life by considering the end of it—a teaching/prodding/revelation moment not unlike the classic modern day high school assignment that asks students to write their own obituaries. But the New Testament is not the reason these horrifically vivid images of Hell are seared into our collective imaginations. Those are compliments of the gifted allegorical poet Dante in his *Inferno,* written nearly 1400 years later:

> Forsake all hope, you who enter here...Here sighs, complaints, and deep groans, sounded through the starless air...many tongues, a terrible crying, words of sadness, accents of anger, voices deep and hoarse...these wretches, who never truly lived, were naked, and goaded viciously by hornets, and wasps, there, making their faces stream with blood, that mixed with tears, was collected, at their feet, by loathsome worms...muddy people in the fen, naked, and all with the look of anger. They were striking each other, not only with hands, but head, chest, and feet, mangling each other with their teeth, bite by bite...dilated flakes of fire, falling slowly like snow in the windless mountain.[15]

Good stuff. Hard to resist if you are a "fire and brimstone" sort of preacher, even if it does come out of medieval poetry and not Scripture. Some speculate that it was the very silence about the whos and whys and hows of Hell that led people to want to fill in the blanks. The threat of eternal torment just seems to carry more sway than the simple, abundantly generous offer of Grace. Sort of like a parent asking nicely, patiently, lovingly for a child to do something vs. "do it now or you're grounded." Or don't do that, "it'll go on your permanent record!!!" It appears that, perhaps, some discomfort with the notion of placing one's hope in Christ alone led the curious and the superficially pious and those who favor a stick over a carrot approach to enlarge on the statements of Scripture in this way.[16]

If there is one conclusive thing to be said of Hell it is that there is only one sin that condemns a person to eternity there: the rejection of God. Even to a person who doesn't believe in anything but human reason, it makes perfect sense. We say, "I don't believe in God, I don't need God, I don't want anything to do with God," and so God lets us spend eternity in the one place He isn't. Isn't that what we asked for? We just don't see the price, eternally speaking, of our request. But Dante did:

> We were sullen in the sweet air,
> that is gladdened by the sun,
> bearing indolent smoke in our hearts:
> now we lie here, sullen, in the black mire.[17]

Indelible poetic language aside, the essential truth of Hell is fairly simple. And on this virtually all biblical scholars agree: Hell is, ultimately, the absence of God.[18]

HELL
UNLOADED

- The word Jesus uses for Hell refers to an actual earthly place.

- *Gehenna* is how Jesus demonstrates the inevitable result of harming other people and communities.

- Hell is the desperation man experiences whenever he feels he's been left for scrap.

- Hell is ultimately the absence of God.

Study Questions
HELL

1. Do you hear people use the word *Hell* often in the culture? What do you think people mean when they use this word? What do you think Christians mean when they use this word?

2. *Sheol* Is the Hebrew word we have translated as *Hell* in English. On pages 46-47, what are some of the descriptions you read about Sheol in this chapter?

3. According to the authors, on pages 47-48, who first tied Hades (Hell) to the notion of a location for the unrighteous?

4. On pages 49 we read: *gehenna* is the word Jesus uses that we have translated as Hell in English. Where is *gehenna* and what did it represent?

5. Read Matthew 5:21-22. As you read on page 50, this is the first time Jesus uses the word *gehenna*. What is the point he is making here? What is the offense that has been committed and is punishable by a sentence to Hell?

6. According to the authors, on page 54, what is the
    one sin that condemns a person to Hell? Why
    does this make sense?

7. In the final paragraph we read: Indelible poetic
    language aside, the essential truth of Hell is fairly
    simple. And on this virtually all biblical scholars
    agree: Hell is ultimately the _____.
    What do you think it would mean to live this
    way?

Chapter 5

SATAN

Early on in the movie *The Devil Wears Prada*, Andy, the smart, anti-fashion heroine, snickers about the attention to detail being given to "this stuff." Meryl Streep, the devilish, fashion omnipower, counters archly, "Oh, I see. You think this stuff has nothing to do with you?" She goes on to weave a tale of strategic decision making through people, choices, time, and garments to explain how the "lumpy blue" discount sweater Andy is wearing—as if to tell people she is above caring about "this stuff"—was actually "chosen for her" by the skillful people in that very room years before.

When it comes to taking the spiritual forces of good and evil seriously, we tend to dismiss it with the same smirking shrug Andy offered her boss. Even practicing Christians will wave off the idea of "spiritual attack," claiming they just don't believe/understand/

accept "that stuff." But, much like the "cerulean" blue color in T*he Devil Wears Prada*, evil does, indeed, have the power to be disseminated through time and people and choices, affecting the lives of countless unsuspecting souls. The stuff of evil is not happenstance; there is a strategic mind behind it, one that applies itself to the building up of evil in the world and—even more critically—to the tearing down of the people who love, or endeavor to love, God. His name is Satan, the Hebrew word for "adversary." And although he may be a great movie villain, he is not fictitious. If you have any interest in going through life with your eyes wide open, there is—ultimately—no way around "this stuff."

As we've seen in other chapters of this book, the image we have today of Satan has progressed over time, cultures, and various writings. It began with a small "s," and did not represent any one being, but simply any force that played an adversarial role.[1] In fact, the very first time the word "adversary" appears is this "…and **the angel of the Lord** took his stand in the way as his adversary (*satan*)" (Numbers 22:22). In other words, God himself uses spiritual "adversaries" to test and/or redirect his people. This seems like shocking news, but it is supported again and again in the Old Testament. In 1 Kings 11:14 it is spelled out clearly that **God raised up** "an adversary" against Solomon. By the time we get to Job, we are finally given a glimpse of how these adversarial agents are commissioned. In this passage, the word Satan—now with a capital "S"—represents "the accuser."

> Now there was a day when the sons of God came to present themselves before the Lord, and Satan also came among them. The Lord said to Satan, "From where have you come?" Satan answered the Lord and said, "From going to and fro on the earth, and from walking up and down on it." And the Lord said to Satan, "Have you considered my servant Job, that there is none like him on the earth, a blameless and upright man, who fears God and turns away from evil?" Then Satan answered the Lord and said, "Does Job fear God for no reason? Have you not put a hedge around him and his house and all that he has, on every side? You have blessed the work of his hands, and his possessions have increased in the land. But stretch out your hand and touch all that he has, and he will curse you to your face." And the Lord said to Satan, "Behold, all that he has is in your hand. Only against him do not stretch out your hand." So Satan went out from the presence of the Lord (Job 1:6-12).

Satan wastes no time in destroying Job's servants, property, livestock, and children. In response, Job drops to his knees, head shaven, and cries out these most faithful of words, "Naked I came from my mother's womb, and naked shall I return. The Lord gave, and the Lord has taken away; blessed be the name of the Lord" (Job 1:21). Thus begins the now infamous story of "the suffering of Job." What most fail to remember—because, really, who wants to believe it—is that it is God who *allows* Satan to mess with Job to test his faithfulness. Modern ears cannot abide by this kind of God. But God's ways are not our ways.

It might be worthwhile to take a moment here to consider, in your own heart and mind, why God might allow a good and faithful servant like Job to be tested. Was it for his own good? For the good of the community? For all of humanity—both then and now? If he knew then what we know now about Jesus Christ—the ultimate suffering servant—would Job, do you imagine, let God test him all over again?

Whatever our answers, the fact remains: God keeps Satan "on staff" in the role of the adversary/ the accuser/the opponent. Perhaps it's as simple as "keeping your friends close and your enemies closer." Or maybe God uses Satan as the original "devil's advocate," providing a counterpoint for His benevolent eye as He considers the comings and goings of His people. All possible, but Scripture directs us to a more challenging truth: that the Creator of the Universe considers it necessary—for now—for the Good that comes from God to have a polar opposite. The narrative of human history, as Scripture reveals, is being written in flesh on the battlefield of good and evil. "If the "character" of Satan is not cast," as R.C.H. Lenski teaches, "then man himself is converted into his own devil."[2]

Think about it. If there must be a force for evil **in this world** then God would never neglect to fill it. He knows us too well. Knows that if He leaves the greatest villain role of all times up for grabs that one of us—ok, lots of us—will clamber to rise to it. (Can't you just see the reality shows now? The S Factor. American Evil. The Real House-Devils of Las Vegas.) No. If God has a reason for there to be rulers of dueling kingdoms, then He created—and oversees—them both.

This notion of "dualism" is well supported, even in the secular realm. Newton's Third Law of motion, for example—for every action there is an equal and opposite reaction—reinforces the premise that if the universe possesses a powerful force for Good, then it must also possess a powerful force for Bad. The Chinese Philosophy of yin-yang embodies this same dualistic idea: light and dark, hot and cold, male and female, etc. They see these pairings not so much as adversarial but as complementary, forming a dynamic system in which the whole is greater than the parts.

Is it possible, then, that God sees evil as "complementary" to the good as He implements justice and mercy in the world? We can never know the mind of God, but we can clearly see his hand in allowing Satan to act, and in the progression of *satan* from merely an opponent to a capital "S" superbeing principally identified with the "evil inclination" and with the "angel of death."[3]

By the time Jesus enters the scene, we are seeing in nearly equal measure two Greek words that mean accuser or opponent: *diabolos* (devil) and *satanas* to designate the Being who lures to evil and opposes God's people.[4] In addition, we see the term *Beelzebul* which in its various forms may be translated as lord "of the flies," "of the dung," "of the idol," or "of enmity."[5] And although we would like to sequester this figure off in some distant, scary, theatrical "Hell," as we learned in the last chapter, that is not where we find Satan.

The Dead Sea Scrolls, the cultural and religious writings of the ancient Jewish people of Qumran, also reveal a philosophical foundation of opposite ideas: righteousness and lawlessness, believing and unbelieving, temple of God and temples of idols, to name a few. Both in these Qumran scrolls as well as throughout the New Testament, Satan is the opposite of Christ. He considers himself to be the "prince of **this world**."[6] Not of Hell—of Here and Now. With us. Tempting us, just as he did to Jesus at the beginning of his ministry.

"Then Jesus was led up by the Spirit into the wilderness to be tempted by the devil" (Matthew 4:1).

Well, sure, but that's Jesus. He had to be tempted, right? God had to make sure he was ready for the crucifixion and everything. But what would Satan want with regular folks like us?

Isn't it obvious? If you're skipping through life with little thought of God or neighbor, the adversary is going to do everything he can to keep you on that path. And if you're walking with God—or trying to—he's going to double-down and do everything he can to tempt you off the "narrow way." Could this be why The Lord's Prayer says: **"And lead us not into temptation"**? There it is. Right in the prayer we say so often we forget what it means. **Lead us not.** Why? Because we're scared we won't pass the test. That we won't be able to do what Jesus did, what Job did, to stand unwavering in our faith as the world is upended around us. No, we suspect we will be more like Peter when he boasts of his undying love for Christ and then, within hours, denies him three times. We wish we could be sure we'd do better, but just in case, we skip clinging to the next line **"But deliver us from the evil one."** [7] In other words, God, just don't let anything bad happen to us. Ever. Please.

This is likely the sort of thinking that underlies the rapidly growing "spiritual but not religious" movement. Stripping it down to the major identifiers, "spiritual but not religious" people are those who want to believe there's something sort of magical and powerful and supernatural like God—and they certainly want Him on their side—but don't want to associate with any people or organizations or ideas that seem bad or narrow or judgmental; in other words, The Church. They believe He can do good things for them, rescue them, keep them from being too shallow, but they don't want to get into all the other mess—sin, the devil, what men and woman are supposed to do and be to each other. But they like candles and incense and the little fluttery feelings one gets when you hear a child sing in church. Things that don't conflict with the fluttery feelings their friends get from other kinds of candles and incense. You know, spiritual things.

Ironically, the spiritual realm to which so many people now ascribe is filled with as many demons as angels. They work through Psychics and Tarot Card readers, to be sure, but also through unscrupulous bosses and YOLO-psychology, and friends who tempt you to have just one more glass of wine. Evil can trickle down through the fears of parents and the seemingly benevolent desire to "do right by your kids." Satan starts the temptations by raising a cloud of doubt about right, wrong, and where we draw the line.[8] Then, inch by inch and app by app, he changes the very sea of input in which we swim, making what was once unseemly or nefarious the new normal. (Toddlers in skull t-shirts? Why not?!) Satan has been at this a long time.

Predictably, then, of all the wretched havoc he wreaks in the world, there's nothing he likes more than to derail a good and faithful servant of the Lord. And here's the hardest part of all; God may let him try. We see it again as Jesus warns his disciple just before Simon Peter's infamous denials. "Simon, Simon, behold, Satan *demanded* (also translated as "has obtained permission") to have you, that he might sift you like wheat, but I have prayed for you that your faith may not fail" (Luke 22:31-32). Later, in the same passage, as Jesus reaches the Mount of Olives and nears his devastating fate, he asks the apostles to pray *not for him*, but for themselves. "Pray that you may not enter into temptation" (v. 40). Not long after, when He chastises them for falling asleep He says "Rise and Pray," but—again—it is *not for him*, but for themselves, "that you may not enter into temptation" (v. 46). As believers, then, this is our daily work: to pray that we are not led into temptation. That Satan does not tap God on the shoulder and say "what about that one?" And that, if he does, if we should be pushed to the point of breaking, that we will continue to cry out, as Job did, as Jesus did, "Father, into your hands, I commend my spirit," and leave the rest to Him.

No wonder people want to be spiritual but not religious. Or nothing at all. I mean, who wants to deal with all "this stuff." But like it or not, this is **the truth** of the universe. We can ignore it or avoid it or dismiss it, but we cannot make it not so. Satan will continue to use demons and mortals to win what he can. God will continue to grant him permission, on occasion, to test his beloved. And Jesus Christ, the one who conquered death and the devil **for all time**, will have the final say. There is no other way. "For human nature is far too weak to resist the devil by its own strength. He holds everyone captive who has not been set free through faith. Against the Devil the power of Christ is needed."[9]

C.S. Lewis reminds us of this Power in *The Silver Chair* when Jill, dying of thirst, approaches the stream where the Lion, that is Christ, stands watch. She seeks his assurance that he will not "consume" her if she dares inch closer to the cool, fresh water. He makes no assurances. The gurgling sounds cry out to her parched soul but she is unable to overcome her fear that this water will somehow lead her to become something she can't imagine—or control. "I suppose I must go and look for another stream then," she says. To which the Lion matter-of-factly responds, "There is no other stream."[10]

There is no other stream. Is it any wonder, then, that as Jesus began his ministry, Satan appears on the scene with such a vengeance? Were Jesus not the enemy of Satan, why would Satan have bothered? All throughout the Gospels, Satan works at a fever pitch. We see him in Peter who is setting his mind "not on divine things but on human things" (Matthew 16:23). We see him in a possessed man named Legion—"for we are many"—who recognizes, and is instantly threatened by Jesus the "Son of the Most High God" (Mark 5:7). We see him snatching the word out of the hearts of those "on the path" (Mark 4:15), and holding an old woman in physical bondage (Luke 13:16). We see him as "the thorn in the flesh," of Paul, ensuring that he will never feel "too elated" in his ministry (2 Cor. 12:7). We see him enter Judas (Luke 22:3), and the heart of Ananias, who lied about his contributions to the church (Acts 5:3).

In fact, one of the places Satan delights most in appearing is, sadly, but predictably, The Church.[11] In the Parable of the Wheat and the Weeds (Matthew 13:24-30) Jesus explains that the presence of evil in the community is due to the activity of the Enemy. It is impossible, the parable teaches, for The Church—the universal church or any church on any street corner—to ever be absolutely pure.[12] Those who are following Christ and those who are doing the bidding of Satan within Christ's Body will be sorted out on the last day. Until then, we may take comfort in the wisdom of St. John: "The light shines in the darkness, and the darkness has not overcome it" (John 1:5).

Let us close the chapter on Satan with the words that God has given us for the spiritual battle. We find many ways to misuse this passage, most often to amp ourselves up for some big social or political battle. But let us read it now with fresh eyes, and see if, perhaps, what it is telling us most of all is that **Satan is real**, and that we are to pray "without ceasing" that we may stand firm whenever tempted.

Finally, be strong in the Lord and in the strength of his might. Put on the whole armor of God, that you may be able to stand against the schemes of the devil. For we do not wrestle against flesh and blood, but against the rulers, against the authorities, against the cosmic powers over this present darkness, against the spiritual forces of evil in the heavenly places. Therefore take up the whole armor of God, that you may be able to withstand in the evil day, and having done all, so stand firm (Ephesians 6:10-13).

And remember that, above all, Satan is a Liar. When he lies he speaks according to his own nature.[1] And the biggest lie of all is that you shouldn't take "this Jesus stuff" too seriously.

---

[1] John 8:44

SATAN
UNLOADED

- Satan means the adversary, accuser or opponent.

- He is not a metaphor; he is both real and supernatural.

- His purpose is to promote evil in the world and to tempt God's people.

- Satan is the father of lies.

Study Questions
SATAN

1. Do you think most Christians believe in Satan? What do you think non-Christians think about Satan?

2. READ Numbers 22:15-35. On page 60, we read the Hebrew word *satan* translates as what word in English? From the scripture reading, who are the important characters in this story? In verses 20-21 what goes wrong? How does God intervene? In verse 35 what is the parting reminder?

3. On page 63 we read scholar R.C.H. Lenski's suggestion for why Satan exists. What does he say?

4. According to the authors, on page 64, where does Satan reside? Of what realm does he consider himself to be the prince?

5. On pages 65 & 69 the authors detail both when and where Satan works hardest to tempt people. When and Where? Why do you think this is important to understand?

6. What are some subtle, seemingly innocuous examples of temptation that Satan has used on you or a loved one? Can you imagine ways in which those small temptations lead to bigger problems?

7. On page 68 we read, Satan becomes very active when Jesus enters the scene to start his ministry. Does this support the idea that Satan is the _____ of Jesus? Why?

8. READ John 8:44. The final paragraph of the chapter says: And remember that, above all, Satan is a _____. When he lies he speaks according to _____. And the biggest lie of all is _____. What do you think about this?

Chapter 6

SAVED

"Are you or are you not a member of the Communist party?" This was the defining identity question that rippled through the hearts and minds and black & white TVs of America in the early 1950s, setting off a wave of fear, alienation, and jingoism. Twenty years later, a new and equally divisive question began to fan out across the nation—through fellowship halls and bar-b-cues and beauty parlors—rising up from the lips of gregarious Christians seeking to elicit the new private handshake of personal salvation. "Are you saved?" they began to ask most anyone who would listen. Some responded with fear and "fell in line"—or tried to. But many in the larger culture looked on with bemused contempt. The question seemed to reveal as much about the needy zeal of the person asking than about any deep concern they had for the respondent. "Are you saved?" resounded like judgment, not grace. Like the sort of

cliquish insider badges we start trying to earn in grade
school and carry into adulthood with our zip codes, cars,
and   academic   credentials—only   now   these   new
Christians seemed to be racking up bonus points on some
heavenly gold star chart. "Are you saved?" they raised
their children to ask, leading to satirical movies like
Saved. This 2004 sleeper comedy is described on the
Internet Movie Database (IMDB): "*When a girl attending
a Christian high school becomes pregnant, she finds
herself ostracized and demonized, as all of her former
friends turn on her.*" Hypocrisy not mercy. This is what
the word *saved* soon came to look like to those outside
The Church. Is it any wonder, then, that they ran from
Christianity?

Whether or not we personally have ever asked
someone about their salvation, all Christians now swim in
a culture where the word is viewed as something of a
punchline. How, then, are we to turn the tide? Well, we
can start by being aware that if we make *salvation* solely
about the afterlife, we are doing a grave disservice to the
full blessing of the word. So, too, if we remain unclear on
what the gift of salvation is all about, reciting the words
without embodying an understanding of the grand
narrative. If we are to be able to "give a reason for the
hope that we have," we should begin by remembering
this simple truth: God is the source of salvation. In the
old covenant, he saved people and nations physically. In
the new covenant, he saves them spiritually and eternally.[1]

When Jewish people say "Shalom" or Christians offer "the peace of the Lord," they sum up nicely the spirit with which the Hebrew *hosia* and Greek *sōzō*—both verbs for *saved*—are intended: we are at peace with Him, at peace with ourselves, at peace with our brothers and sisters, at peace with the finite nature of our earthly lives. In both, there is a holistic view of both the physical and spiritual healing that God bestows on humans.[2] The Latin word *salvere* captures a similar meaning: "to be well, in good health." It was so much a part of the zeitgeist of the ancient world that the common greeting on the street was *Salve!* In the Middle Ages the echoes of the word's divinity were reclaimed in the formal Mass with the *Salve Regina* prayers. Hail, Mary, Full of Grace!

So how did the "*saved*" that connotes peace and wholeness—both very "translatable" and desirable contemporary ideals—come to mean nothing more than "do you or do you not have a ticket to heaven?" People. Time. Ignorance. Sin. Spin. You know, baggage.

What does the word *saved* mean to you? If you're not 100% clear, you're in good company. An informal study done by a psychologist/theologian asked only one question: What are we saved from? Only one in ten—including regular churchgoers—could answer with confidence or accuracy. Formal studies certainly support this. In a multi-denominational Barna Group Report on issues related to salvation, justification, works righteousness, and the Gospel, Christians across all demographic categories proved to be sorely lacking in the basic understanding of salvation that Martin Luther gave his life for: **That we are justified by grace through faith**. As Paul wrote to the Ephesians, "For by grace you have been saved through faith, and this is not your own doing; it is the gift of God—not the result of works, so that no one may boast" (Ephesians 2:8-9).

Here we highlight the answers of Lutheran Christians, not because they fared any worse than the other groups, but because the doctrine of *Grace Alone, Faith Alone, Scripture Alone* is their whole foundation. And, well, if any group should know the answer to these basic theological questions, they should. Over 6000 adults were asked:

- If a good person could *earn* their way to heaven? 54% of Lutherans said yes;
- If people can *only* be justified before God by loving others? Nearly half of all Lutherans agreed/probably agreed. Only 20% disagreed;
- If the *main emphasis* of the Gospel is on God's rules for right living? Over 60% of Lutherans agreed that the Gospel is primarily about rules. "If most Lutherans understand the Gospel to be simply a code of conduct, then Luther's teachings about salvation by grace through faith

have   been   superseded   by   moral legalism."[3]

This should be a wake-up call for all Christians. If we want to restore our understanding of sound teaching so that we might be able to share the Good News with others, we need to begin at the beginning: how the Hebrews heard the word *saved* (*yāša'*). Forms of this word are used over 350 times. It has an Arabic foundation that means to "make wide" or "make sufficient." This stands in direct opposition to their word for narrow (*ṣārar*), meaning to "be restricted" or "cause distress."[4] These ideas were all incorporated into the primary word for *salvation* (*yosha'*), which was understood as a "broadening" or "enlarging."

When you consider that most secular people in contemporary American culture view the Christian faith as something that makes things tighter, smaller, and more rigid, you can see how far we've drifted from the source. This drift seems to be tied to an imbalance in our application of Law and Gospel, or, for some groups, in a complete lopping off of the ongoing role of the Old Testament in the salvific history of God and mankind.

Long before the salvation offered to all through Jesus Christ, there was the salvation offered to God's chosen people in Exodus. The word Exodus literally means "a way out." Chillingly, this is the phrase most commonly used by suicidal people—they simply can't see "a way out." *The* way out. This is the salvation that God alone provides.

A review of the broad, 3-point story arc of Exodus will help us put our thinking about rules and grace back in proper alignment. First, *God* leads his people out of slavery in Egypt—the most powerful empire in the ancient world at that time. Next, *God* establishes His presence, distinguishing His people from all other peoples on earth. Finally, *God* reconstitutes them as a people—for His name—at the foot of Mount Sinai.

The last was the single most difficult. Why? Here were people who knew only slavery in Egypt for centuries, to whom God was now about to give identity, purpose, and structure. To accomplish this *God*:

- had to form them into an army of warriors who could conquer the land promised to their ancestors;
- had to form them into a community that could live together in the desert and eventually the promised land;
- needed to provide direction on **how to be** God's people—through their relationships with God and with each other.[5]

So what does God do first? He doesn't give them rules. He doesn't tell them to start fighting. No, first He saves. "Then the Lord said, I have surely seen the affliction of my people who are in Egypt and have heard their cry because of their taskmasters. I know their sufferings and I have come down to deliver them out of the hand of the Egyptians and to bring them up out of that land to a good and broad land, a land flowing with milk and honey,..." (Exodus 3:7-8).

Contemporary readers and HBO viewers will find a good metaphoric example of this rescuing in the fictional series of medieval power plays, *Game of Thrones*. Many Christians may steer clear of the show because of its graphic sex and violence, or its unorthodox blending of religious and pagan motifs, but the culture does not. Those who do watch the show with "the mind of Christ" can learn a great deal not only about the sinfulness of the human heart but also its desire for salvation. And, in certain characters, particularly the exiled princess Daenerys Targaryen, how one might speak to modern listeners about salvation. Once enslaved as well, Daenerys (pronounced da-nair-ee-us) comes to unexpected power over a scant tribe of the lowly in a remote desert. From there, she begins to build a new people by freeing the slaves of despotic rulers. In the climactic scene of an episode aptly called "Breaker of Chains," thousands of her now-amassed troops of freed men face off with a legion of enslaved soldiers who have the physical advantage, poised high behind the battlements of a great fortress. She has offered them freedom, but they cannot believe her promise. In a dramatic and startling sign to them, her soldiers catapult what appears to be a violent barrage of cannonfire over the ramparts. The wooden canisters burst open revealing their contents: the broken shackles of Daenerys's warriors, the ones who stand behind her, willingly, to fight for freedom in the land.

First God saves. Then God provides.

Why does it matter that we know and embody these Old Testament narratives? Because they lead us to the cross, not only in deed and truth but in the very root of the word. From *saved* and *salvation* we move to *Savior.* Have you been noticing how similar the word Joshua—from the Hebrew *yosha'*—is to the name Jesus? They both mean Savior, as does Yahweh, which shares the same root.[6] Like a single strand of DNA that reveals the make-up of an entire life, we can see the throughline of salvation history in this one small word: *savior.* We see how it maintains its essence even as it spreads through time and nations:

From the first use in 2 Samuel 22:3:

> "My God, my rock, in whom I take refuge, my shield, and the horn of my salvation, my stronghold and my refuge, my **savior**…"

Through its embattled history of deliverance as typified in 2 Kings 13:5:

> "Therefore the LORD gave Israel a **savior**, so that they escaped from the hand of the Syrians..."

To Mary's joyful claim in Luke 1:47 as she receives the divine Call to bear His Son:

> "My spirit rejoices in God my **Savior**."

To the tender wisdom passed from Paul to his 'beloved child" Timothy about the God:

> "Who **saved us** and called to a holy calling, not because of our works but because of his own purpose and grace, which he gave us in Christ Jesus before the ages began, and which has now been manifested through the appearing of our **Savior** Christ Jesus, who abolished death and brought life and immortality to light through the gospel" (2 Timothy 1:9-10).

To the final use in Jude 1:25:

> "To the only God our **Savior** through Jesus Christ our Lord be glory, majesty,

dominion and authority before all time
now and forever! Amen."

The very name of Jesus reveals that he is the
Savior, one with God and His Word before all time. So
what does the *Christ* add? Christ, from the Greek
christos, came to mean "the anointed one" (more on this
later). This is how we come to confess with both
confidence and faith that Jesus Christ is the anointed
Savior of the world, and that "Everyone who calls on the
name of the Lord shall be **saved**" (Romans 10:13). In a
single, bloody instant, he paid the price for the sins of the
world. In a single, mysterious ascension, the corporate
salvation of the Old Testament became the personal
salvation of the New. Paul unites them—the old and the
new—as he teaches that our salvation is lived out **in this
world** "in Christ." Each believer is both in union with the
risen Lord in a personal and direct way, as well as being
connected to all believers in the Body of Christ—not only
those who live with us now, but for all time.

A deeper knowledge of the Word will, we hope,
be helpful, but a vigilant self-awareness of how we hear
and use language may be the most useful tool of all.
Remember, in the same way that sin makes us turn in on
ourselves, a misuse of the true meaning of *saved* tends to
make us restrict and exclude. Salvation is, at its very root,
a broadening and enlarging. Think arms wide open,
minds wide open, nets wide open. This is the image that

will keep us in right relation to the heart of the word *saved*.

There are—and may always be—key doctrinal issues about salvation that keep believers within the universal Body at odds. Chief among them: the role of baptism and good works in salvation, and the debates over predestination. These issues will certainly not be addressed in this slim volume, but we find some wisdom for our struggles in the words of German theologian Herman Sasse: "There is actually more unity of the church present where Christians of differing confession honorably determine that they do not have the same understanding of the gospel than where the painful fact of confessional splintering is hidden behind a pious lie."[7]

In other words, hold true to what you believe, yes, but never lose sight of the fact that God continues to see us as one Church—His Church—and trust that He will bring the truth of right understanding to the light in His time. Above all, let us never take lightly the **very high cost** of playing up our differences loudly and contentiously in the public sphere. Those who are offended by this behavior—which is more people than not—may be pushed further away from the very gift you're hoping to help lead them to.

"Are you saved?" By now we should be clear that this is not a box to be checked off, but the ultimate matter of life and death between each individual and their

Creator. We, who have been given eyes to see, were not called to be Gate Keepers but Messengers on the sidewalks and corridors of our earthly lives. Our place is not to ask, or to judge, but to share, with Paul's example as our guide. "When I am with those who are weak, I share their weakness, for I want to bring the weak to Christ. Yes, I try to find common ground with everyone, doing everything I can to save some" (1 Corinthians 9:22, New Living Translation). If we wonder or worry about another person's salvation, let us start by remembering our own:

> *Amazing Grace, how sweet the sound,*
> *That saved a wretch like me.*
> *I once was lost but now am found,*
> *Was blind, but now I see.*[8]

It is from this place of humility and gratitude that we can approach a person who may not know Christ, wanting nothing more than to be in some small way a *salve* to their deepest pains and shames and unrequited longings. Somehow in the mess and blessing of these encounters, we trust that by the grace of God—and God alone—we may one day lean shoulder to shoulder with them to sing those great words together.

SAVED
UNLOADED

- Saved is not about a "ticket to Heaven."

- Saved is being at peace with God, ourselves, and others.

- The name Jesus literally means Savior.

- Salvation is a broadening, enlarging, arms-wide-open word.

Study Questions
SAVED

1. Do you think you are *saved*? If you ask someone if they are *saved*, how do you imagine it makes them feel?

2. According to page 76, is salvation solely about the afterlife?

3. Reading page 77, when we consider the Hebrew, Greek, and Latin words—*hosia, sōzō, salvere*—what do these words mean? How do these definitions align with your own personal thought about being saved?

4. According to the authors, on page 80, what is the 3-point story arc of Exodus? Next, the authors ask the question "What does God do first?" READ Exodus 3:7-8. How many chapters in Exodus do you have to move through before God gives the 10 Commandments? Why is this important to know? What does it make you think about salvation?

5. On page 82 we read, Joshua, *yosha'*, and Jesus all
    share the same Hebrew root. What is the root
    word in English?

6. On page 84 we read, salvation is, at its very root,
    a _____ . Think   arms
    _____ , minds _____ , nets
    _____ . This is the image that will
    keep us in right relation to the heart of the word
    saved. How does this definition relate to God's
    saving work?

7. If we wonder or worry about another person's
    salvation, let us start by remembering our own.
    How do the opening four lines of the song
    Amazing Grace influence your thoughts about
    your salvation? How about the salvation of
    others?

Chapter 7

CONFESS

Quick: what's the first thing that comes to your mind when you hear the word *confess*? Someone walking into the police station to turn himself in? A movie scene played out in the confessional in the far corner of an empty church? These are the two most common ways the culture knows and thinks of the word, which tells us that 1) *confess* has come to be synonymous with admitting you've done something bad, and 2) the admission is to be made to a person(s) who will then decide how bad you are and the price you should pay for what you've done. This is all well and good when it comes to the civic/judicial use of the word, but in spiritual terms it's not only narrow, it's disastrous. Would you ever tell someone that the *definition* of the word *love*, for example, is "getting into fights and making up?" Of course not. But this is the level of error we perpetuate when we allow people to think that the full and proper use of *confession* in the context of the church is nothing more than rattling off a litany of our sin and shame and guilt.

How, then, can we begin to hear—and therefore share—the word *confess* as it was first given to us? It may help to remember that the word is introduced in Leviticus, and that one of the main sources of that book is the material from the "Holiness School." Don't you just love that name? From the beginning, our behavior in relationship to God and neighbor was seen as something we would need to learn; a process in which mistakes would be made, encouragement offered, forgiveness provided lavishly, wisdom gained, and people made more fit to live with one another and at peace in their own skin as they were daily freed of the burden of their less than stellar behavior. *Confess,* in Hebrew *yādâ*,[1] makes its first appearance after Moses reviews a list of common—and often oblivious—missteps and how each person is to address them, ending with

> When any of you utter aloud a rash oath for a bad or good purpose, whatever people utter in an oath, and are unaware of it, when you come to know it, you shall in any of these be guilty. When you realize your guilt in any of these you shall confess the sin that you have committed (Leviticus 5:4-5 NRSV).

The fact that other parts of the chapter reference "guilt offerings" of various animals and rituals involving the temple priest make many—perhaps even most—in contemporary culture dismiss the wisdom and relevance of these verses outright. But let's think about what Moses just said. Basically, if you blurt something out without really meaning it, you're going to be guilty, as in, you're going to feel badly about it later, and wish you had some way to not feel badly anymore. Need a contemporary example? How about…"I'll call you." If we think we don't feel "guilty" when we offer up that phrase insincerely, just think about how we react the next time we run into the person we said it to.

With these ground rules firmly established, *confess* quickly grows to express its full and primary biblical meaning which incorporates *to praise, give thanks, extol, acknowledge,* and *proclaim.*[2] Simply put, *to confess* is to return each day to the Hebrew prayer, the great Shema, "*Hear, Oh Israel, the Lord is our God, the Lord alone. You shall love the Lord your God with all your heart, and with all your soul, and with all your might*" (Deuteronomy 6:4-6). Recognizing our sins is just part of the process of loving God, the part that—ironically—leads to freedom and joy:

> Blessed is the one whose transgression
> is forgiven,
> whose sin is covered.
> Blessed is the man against whom the LORD counts

no iniquity,
and in whose spirit there is no deceit.
For when I kept silent, my bones wasted away
through my groaning all day long.
For day and night your hand was heavy
upon me;
my strength was dried up as by the heat of
summer. *Selah*
I acknowledged my sin to you,
and I did not cover my iniquity;
I said, "I will confess my transgressions
to the LORD,"
and you forgave the iniquity of my sin. *Selah*
(Psalm 32:1-5)

Or, as they say in the 12-step world, "You're only as sick as your secrets."

The full sweep of the word was made immortal by Augustine whose tell-all memoir, *The Confessions*, is one of the most widely read books of all time. For those who think of church people as being somehow different from the general population—either squeaky clean or horrifically hypocritical—Augustine will come as a revelation. "Loving and being loved were sweet to me, the more so if I could also enjoy a lover's body," he tells us of his college years in the early 4th century. "The mind commands the body, and is instantly obeyed; the mind commands itself and meets with resistance," he notes, as he struggles to understand the battle between the will and

the spirit. And he defines with glorious humor how those
struggles play out as he endeavors to move closer to a life
of prayer: "Grant me chastity and self-control, but please
not yet."

Augustine's eight timeless chapters of confession
recount his journey from boyhood, when he first
recognizes the evil that dwells in each man as he steals
recklessly from a pear tree: "This fruit was not enticing,
either in appearance or in flavor…we derived pleasure
from the deed simply because it was forbidden."
Throughout his twenties he notes that, "I and others like
me were seduced and seducers, deceived ourselves and
deceivers of others amid a welter of desires; publicly
through the arts reputed "liberal," and secretly under the
false name of religion"—namely, the power of rhetoric,
the lure of astrology, and the delight in belittling
Christians. All the while, there was the whisper and itch
and tug of God, calling him to Himself. After a lifetime
of Augustine's rejecting and denying, God met him in the
Garden where in the throws of brokenness he hears a
voice singing as if it were a nursery rhyme, "Pick it up
and read, pick it up and read, pick it up and read." So he
picked up the Bible beside him and read the first passage
his eyes met: "Not in dissipation and drunkenness, nor in
debauchery and lewdness, nor in arguing and jealously;
but put on the Lord Jesus Christ, and make no provision
for the flesh or the gratification of your desires" (Romans
13:13). And that, as they say, was that.[3]

If we ever forget the full meaning of the word *confession*, we need only pick up the wholly secular *Cliff Notes* for Augustine's book:

> The word "confession" has several senses, all of which operate throughout the work. Confession can mean admitting one's sins, which Augustine does with gusto, confessing not only his ambition and his lust but also his intellectual pride, his misplaced faith in Manichaeism, and his misunderstanding of Christianity. Confession also means a statement of belief, and this aspect is reflected in Augustine's detailed account of how he arrived at his Christian beliefs and his knowledge of God. Finally, confession means a statement of praise, and in the *Confessions,* Augustine constantly gives praise to the God who mercifully directed his path and brought him out of misery and error. In essence, the *Confessions* is one long prayer.[4]

Augustine went on to become a priest, a bishop, and one of the most prolific writers and defenders of the early church. Still, his *Confessions* are not timeless because of his "celebrity," but because of his candor. This is how the word *confess* applies to you and me.

Our confession is our statement of *who we are,* *what we believe* and *why we believe* it when it comes to the "meaning of life." This is something that any adult should be able to do but, unfortunately, many—even practicing Christians—cannot. The watershed book about the loss of community in the U.S., *Bowling Alone,* references the work of an expert in Baby Boomer culture. "What distinguishes this generation most is what it does *not* like or does *not* do, and not what it likes or does" (*emphasis ours*).[5] And this "void" in the center of things has, understandably, been passed down to our Millennial children.

In 1966, for example, 86% of college freshmen said that developing a meaningful philosophy of life was essential or very important; in 2014, the number was less than half that.[6] In other words, the majority of the next generation is not only lacking in a philosophy of meaning and truth by which they navigate their lives, they no longer even recognize the need to have one. When we have nothing in particular to tether us, we are, essentially, adrift, glomming onto whatever issue of the day or passing treatise on transcendence comes our way. This ephemeral, anything-goes stance is most misleading to the people who hold it. As Ralph Waldo Emerson said, "People do not seem to realize that their opinion of the world is also a confession of their character."

But how in the world are people to believe anything when there are so many things to choose from?

This is the kicker: when it comes to Jesus Christ, we don't choose. We simply respond to what God has already hard-wired us to know and be and believe. "The word is near you, in your mouth and in your heart" (Romans 10:8). On your lips, as in, right there on the tip of your tongue. All we have to do is remember—not choose—but remember, drawing on that deep well of truth at the very core of our being. Remembering is, not coincidentally, a second Hebrew word (*zākar*) that is translated as confess.[7] *Remember, think about, meditate upon, pay attention to, recollect.* This is the process by which the knowledge of who we are as children of God moves from our heart to our lips and out into the confession of our daily lives.

Which brings us to Jesus and the Gospel and the Greek word most often translated confess, *homologeō*. Although a technical definition would be to "say the same thing," the essence of the word is "to echo back what you have heard."[8] The modern psychotherapy movement uses this basic principle in teaching couples and families and co-workers to interact, learning first to listen, then to state back, "What I hear you saying is…" This is the way in which God wants to communicate with us; we cry out to Him, He hears our prayers, He offers wisdom, guidance, forgiveness, and we respond—we *confess*—that "what I hear you saying, God, is this…". *Homologeō* is the original a-ha moment. This is the primary way the word is used all throughout the New Testament, as seen in this seminal statement of faith: "If you *confess* with your mouth that Jesus is Lord and believe in your heart that God raised him from the dead, you will be saved" (Romans 10:9).

So how is it that a word so simple and pure as this came to be so badly misconstrued? Lots of reasons, but certainly, there was a turning point in the Middle Ages when new dictionaries began listing as the primary and secondary meanings for confess: 1) "to tell or make known (as something wrong or damaging to oneself); admit 2) to acknowledge (sin) to God or to a priest.[9] These subtle (and not so subtle) shifts were part and parcel of the growing power within the church that began—or so it seemed to Martin Luther—to take people further from the truth of Scripture.

Now, trying to get even wise and thoughtful people to make the exact same confession about Divine Truth is like herding cats—or redirecting mules. That's why it's something of a miracle that the Apostle's Creed has arrived in the 21st century intact. This creed, shown here in an early draft from the late 2nd/early 3rd century, lays out the foundation of what every Christian confesses (even if they belong to a church that doesn't believe in creeds *or* confessing).[10]

> I believe in God the Father almighty,
> Creator of heaven and earth.
> I believe in Jesus Christ, His only Son,
> our Lord

He was conceived by the power of the
Holy Spirit,
And born of the Virgin Mary,
He suffered under Pontius Pilate,
was crucified, died, and was buried.
He descended to the dead.
On the third day He rose again.
He ascended into heaven,
and is seated at the right hand of the Father
He will come again to judge the living
and the dead.
I believe in the Holy Spirit,
the holy catholic[11] Church,
the communion of saints,
the forgiveness of sins,
the resurrection of the body,
and the life everlasting. Amen.

There. That's the whole story. Of course, if you're
new to church and you're just sitting there in a pew trying
to figure out what's what and suddenly everyone stands
up and starts reciting this "insider speak" in unison, it
feels very much like a gathering of automatons. For some
it might be just that—rote, perfunctory—but for many,
these words represent what God has spoken to them,
taught them, shown them, done for them, continues to do
and be and call them to become.

Our highly individualized—and seemingly
tolerant—American culture just can't seem to tolerate a

form of spirituality that utilizes corporate language. Funny, because corporate language in the private sector has never in the history of American been so tightly controlled. No spokesperson would dare to get in front of a camera without vetted, pre-scripted talking points. And rare is the corporation that does not adhere to a Brand Standards Manual, the marketing rulebook which dictates wording, font size, color palette, and juxtaposition of all elements, with no deviation allowed. This is so that paid staff with specific expertise won't color outside the lines. Or misspeak in social media. Or misrepresent the mission and values of the Company. The Apostle's Creed is, basically, the Brand Standards Manual for Christianity and, truth be told, it offers a good deal more freedom than, say, the average "non-compete" clause. Confessing this standard aloud is simply one of the ways that people come to hear the story of God's saving work so that they might echo it back in their own lives—not automatically—but sincerely, authentically, and by His grace alone.

This overlap between one's individual relationship to God and one's corporate relationship to the Body is challenged by the Christian tradition of offering up public confession in worship—not the Creed kind, but the reflecting-on-sins kind. Why is this necessary, people wonder? Why not just talk and pray to God privately? And why, if confess means to "echo back what we have heard," do we do it at the beginning of the service, before we've heard the Word of God at all? This matter of placement in liturgy is a question that is worth discussing, but the value of public confession is not. Public confession reminds us in a visible and audible way that we are all in the same boat. The Holy Spirit can use the repentant heart of even one person to set a room on fire with contrition, just as we so often saw in the Old Testament. "O my God, I am ashamed and blush to lift my face to you, my God, for our iniquities have risen higher than our heads, and our guilt has mounted up to the heavens" (Ezra 9:6). Ezra speaks for all, continuing to weep and pray and confess until soon, "the people wept bitterly" (10:1). Sometimes it takes an icebreaker; one person willing to speak the truth to open the clenched hearts of many.

This was the truth that John Wesley acted on when he implemented his own small group model, "The Rules for the Band of Societies," in 1738. According to historical theologian Gary Neal Hansen, these were the four questions that needed to be answered aloud by all members before any other issues were studied or addressed:

1. What known sins have you committed since our last meeting?
2. What temptations have you met with?
3. How were you delivered?
4. What have you thought, said, or done, of which you doubt whether it be sin or not?[12]

That automaton method is sounding pretty good right about now, isn't it? Can we even imagine interacting with our brothers and sisters, and whoever else decides to join the group that day, with this level of forthrightness? Terrifying, yes, but maybe—just maybe—we should try. Because, as Hansen shares, when, as a Body, we take confession seriously we take our faith seriously. We are kept ever humble, we are ever receiving of grace, and we are constantly learning more about discernment, and the subtleties of assessing our own behavior so that we may find greater patience and compassion for others.[13] It is only from that place of naked confession, that we may truly understand and *confess* the Good News of forgiveness in Christ.

What did important voices of the Reformation say about confession? That we are not expected to recite a laundry list of our sins, but rather, daily, to follow the psalmist's advice, "Commit your way to the Lord; trust in him, and he will act" (Psalm 37:5). May this be our confession, now and forevermore.

CONFESS
UNLOADED

- Confessing is an unburdening which leads to freedom.

- Our confession is also a statement of faith.

- Confession includes words of praise directed toward God.

- To confess is to echo back what we hear God saying.

Study Questions
CONFESS

1. At church, when the Pastor asks you to recite a confession of sins or through silent prayer confess to God, what does that confession look like to you? How do you think someone who walks into a church for the first time sees/understands confession?

2. What are some of the definitions of confess we read in this chapter?

3. READ Deuteronomy 6:4-6. What kinds of confession do you see in this prayer?

4. On page 96, this book offers the *Cliff Notes* for St. Augustine's *Confessions*, which include a complete list of all the meanings and nuances of *confess*. What are they?

5. According to the authors, on page 97, our confession is our statement of *who we are*, *what we believe* and *why we believe* it when it comes to the "meaning of life." Briefly describe each of these three components of Christian confession.

Do the 10 Commandments and the Apostle's Creed offer any insight?

6.   READ Romans 10:8-9. According to the authors, on pages 98-99, *Homologeo*—to echo back what you have already heard God say—is the primary definition of the Greek word we have translated as confess in English. Can you describe this concept in your own words?

7.   On page 102 we read "The Rules for the Band of Societies." What if your church or small group required this type of confessing?

8.   What do you think the final paragraph of this chapter is trying to help us understand?

Chapter 8

SUBMIT

On the face of it *submit* is a perfectly ordinary word, one spoken in everyday, non-church conversation more than any other in this book. It has become a "loaded word" in the 21st century because of its use in a handful of Bible passages that speak to the interrelationship of men and women. And, like most things biblical, *submit* picked up its very heavy baggage at a particular moment in time, based on a paradigm shift in the culture: in this case, the era of The Pill and all that it would come to represent about how women regard their sovereignty over their bodies, their lives, and their choices (how's that for a string of loaded words!). And we will get to those verses in due time, but before we can fully understand them, we need to talk about what *submit* really means—both in Scripture and in the world.

The first thing we need to get clear on is that submitting is **always** an act of free will. We choose to do it; it is never imposed on us. Consider the top three definitions in the *Oxford English Dictionary*: 1) *To place oneself* in a position of submission or compliance, 2) *To place oneself* under a certain control or authority; 3) *To surrender oneself* to judgment, correction, treatment, a state of affairs, a condition, etc. When we submit a business proposal to a prospective client, we acknowledge that they have the power to decide whether or not to enlist our services. When we submit to a Breathalyzer or lie detector test we do so because we are hoping to prove our innocence. When we sign our kids up to play Little League, we submit to the rules of the game and the league, and the authority of the coach, who may or may not recognize our child's obvious and considerable talents.

Men who have done time in battle know well what it means to submit to the chain of command for a higher purpose. In the poem "The Charge of the Light Brigade," we are moved by the ideal of those who bravely submit to a valiant death, carrying out orders that are doomed by human error:

> Half a league half a league,
> Half a league onward,
> All in the valley of Death
> Rode the six hundred:
> "Forward, the Light Brigade!

Charge for the guns" he said:
Into the valley of Death
Rode the six hundred.

"Forward, the Light Brigade!"
Was there a man dismay'd?
Not tho' the soldier knew
Some one had blunder'd:
Theirs not to make reply,
Theirs not to reason why,
Theirs but to do & die,
Into the valley of Death
Rode the six hundred...[1]

In the Old Testament, the word or words we translate as *submit* are better understood as *be willing, consent, give allegiance, be busy with or serve, to make a covenant of peace, and even know or have knowledge (of God)*. The very first time the word for *submit* is used is in Genesis 16:9. The story leading up to it speaks volumes about how authority and submission are passed from one to the other in a household for the purpose of **meeting each other's needs** and the greater good.

Now Sarai, Abram's wife, had borne him no children. She had a female Egyptian servant[2] whose name was Hagar. And Sarai said to Abram, "Behold now, the Lord has prevented me from bearing children. Go in to my servant; it may be

that I shall obtain children by her." And Abram listened to the voice of Sarai. So, after Abram had lived ten years in the land of Canaan, Sarai, Abram's wife, took Hagar the Egyptian, her servant, and gave her to Abram her husband as a wife. And he went in to Hagar, and she conceived. And when she saw that she had conceived, she looked with contempt on her mistress. And Sarai said to Abram, "May the wrong done to me be on you! I gave my servant to your embrace, and when she saw that she had conceived, she looked on me with contempt. May the Lord judge between you and me!" But Abram said to Sarai, "Behold, your servant is in your power; do to her as you please." (a better understanding of this translation is "your servant is in your care; do right by her."[3])
 Then Sarai dealt harshly with her, and she fled from her. The angel of the Lord found her by a spring of water in the wilderness, the spring on the way to Shur. And he said, "Hagar, servant of Sarai, where have you come from and where are you going?" She said, "I am fleeing from my mistress Sarai." The angel of the Lord said to her, "Return to

your mistress and **submit** to her
(Genesis 16:1-9).

So, the very first use of *submit* is actually in the
context of two women—the "lady of the house" and her
"personal assistant"—after a sequence of events that
were, to put it mildly, "highly charged." This is when
submission most often comes into play in the world;
when stakes and emotions are running high, and some
previously-agreed-to standard of authority kicks in to
restore order—something of an Emergency Response
System. Hagar failed to submit when she treated Sarai
with disrespect and, later, when she ran off. Sarai failed
to submit when she treated Hagar harshly, and, to a
greater degree, when she refused to believe in, and adhere
to, the timetable God had provided for her own
childbearing. Trust—or the lack thereof—is often at the
heart of these failures.

Of course, the majority of the Old Testament uses
of *submit* are in reference to man and his relationship to
God[4] as typified by Proverb 3:6: "In all your ways *submit*
to him, and he will make your paths straight." As much
as mankind has—and always will—struggle with
submission to God, our contemporary challenges with the
word come not from the Old Testament but the New.

To give us something of a framework to discuss
these ideas, let's start with this: of the nearly 182,000
words in the New Testament, only 40 of them translate as

submit or *subject*. That's a fairly low number when you consider that the Gospel represented the most radical shift in social norms the world had ever known. "There is neither Jew nor Greek, there is neither slave nor free, there is no male and female, for you are all one in Christ Jesus" (Galatians 3:28). In other words, life as you know it will never be the same. All bets are off. No previously acknowledged social order is reliable or enforceable. Wow.

Compare the scope of Christ's call for change to the sort of upheaval experienced in a local church today when someone endeavors to, say, introduce an electric guitar. Let's be honest—all hell breaks loose. And ultimately members—many of them founders of that very church—must decide whether or not to *submit* to the will of the pastor and the new vision or leave the church. Now consider what Peter and Paul were up against as they endeavored to make a new people His church. In the Greco-Roman world the entire economic and social structure was based on the use of slaves, who were considered nothing more than living, breathing property. (As we saw in the Sarai and Abram story, slaves did not even have the right to the children that came out of their own bodies). Free women, in terms of rights, were only slightly higher in the pecking order. They could not own their own land or business. With few exceptions, they were not given an education. They were passed from father to husband in what was, in effect, a business arrangement. Love was not even one of the criteria.[5]

And now this new teaching: that all are one, **all are equal**, all are free in Christ Jesus.

Who do you imagine felt the sting of this Gospel teaching the most? The men, of course, who were not only seeing the playing field leveled before their eyes but were also being given the divine task to "love your wife as Christ loved the church" and to love her as much as you love your own bodies (Ephesians 5:25 & 28). In a deeply entrenched patriarchal culture, where husbands routinely—and without a whiff of condemnation—exercised their right to concubines and slaves, the word of God that Paul was delivering was no doubt heard by many men as both punitive and emasculating. However challenging these verses are for women today, this is likely how hard they were, in the ancient world, for men.[6]

With that in mind, let us look at the most loaded parts of this *submit* verse in its entirety:

> Wives, submit to your own husbands, as to the Lord. For the husband is the head of the wife even as Christ is the head of the church, his body, and is himself its Savior. Now as the church submits to Christ, so also wives should submit in everything to their husbands (Ephesians 5:22-24).

As women join the leadership ranks of Fortune 500 companies and governments and continue to infiltrate and excel in academia, how can we not cringe a little when we hear a phrase like "submit to your husband?" The only way is to breathe deeply the air of the culture in which these verses were written, and keep your eyes on the overarching principle under which these prickly verses fall: "**submit to one another out of reverence for Christ**" (Ephesians 5:21). This, the oft overlooked opening: submit to one another.

In other words, it's mutual. Even a contemporary and wholly secular household can recognize this principle in the pragmatism of "divide and conquer" parenting. One spouse will likely have the "final say" in education, another in finances, one in vacation planning, another in new car selection. In these perfectly ordinary daily exchanges, each is deferring to—submitting to—the expertise, passion, or "authority" of the other. In a healthy relationship, these deferrals are made, for the most part, seamlessly, and to the benefit of both husband and wife.

Submit to one another out of reverence for Christ.

If only Paul had stopped there he could have saved us all a lot of ecclesiastical heartache. But he didn't. Let's keep in mind that the early "Jesus movement" was attracting a lot of women. Women were Paul's fellow workers. Women were prophets and study leaders and hosts of the early house churches. Women were absolutely integral to the early life of the Pauline churches.[7] So how is it that Paul, the egalitarian apostle, came to be the primary voice telling women to submit? Because he was, above all, a shepherd, and as such was tasked with considering the well-being of the whole flock. In the midst of flaring, problematic conflict placing the body of believers and the missional witness at risk, he triages his "management" focus with these priorities at the top of the list: "How is this community treating each other?" and "What does this community of believers look like to outsiders?"[8]

Ephesus, Corinth, Colossae—they were all exhibiting less than Christ-like standards as they tried to understand how to live out the Gospel as a "new family." This epistle we call Ephesians was actually what is known as a "circular letter," with general instructions to many of the early house churches. And although the passages about women submitting are the problematic element for us today, at the time, Paul was preoccupied "primarily with the responsibility of the husband,"[9] and the challenges the men were facing with this new call to mutual submission.

Although Ephesians and others were letters of a general nature, some were more specifically targeted. This was the case in 1 Timothy 2:11 when Paul instructs, "Let a woman learn quietly with all *submissiveness.*" What was going on at the time that would lead Paul to say this? Well, the worshipping community was battling major external threats from secular philosophers, pagan worship, and cultural influence, all informing matters of behavior and dress.[10] Men were quarrelling. Women were parading in provocative, "one uppish" fashions.[11] And a few had assumed unbestowed authority[12]—in other words, jumped ahead without permission faster than prudence, wisdom, or group dynamics would support. Paul asks them to submit, to quietly and politely defer to the subject matter experts within the church, who—due to tradition, education, and culture—were, at the time, primarily men.[13] These comments were not so much based on gender but on behavior.

As we know, radical social change never happens overnight, and forming functional groups of people who work towards a common goal is no cakewalk—even today, even with a few million management and team-building books to consult. The early church had no playbook but Paul. This ongoing need to put out house-church "fires" on the fly is what prompted Paul to put down in parchment the words we now struggle with today. As every leader is called to do from time to time, Paul needed to address some behavior exhibited by specific individuals—both men and women—who were making his job of keeping the *shalom* a whole lot harder. Problem-specific epistles like these are called "occasional letters," which is what Paul wrote to Timothy in response to an occasion or particular challenge, leaving the Church to inherit this loaded verse:

"I do not permit a woman to teach or to exercise *authority* over a man; rather, she is to remain quiet" (1 Timothy 2:11-12, *emphasis ours*).

This verse is somewhat unusual for two primary reasons. The first, Paul does not say "God does not permit," but rather he—"Paul"—does not permit, again supporting the notion that it was a human management decision and not a divine decree. The second, even more unusual; the Greek word translated as *authority* used by Paul in this passage is found **nowhere else** in the entire New Testament. There have been only seven other possible examples of this Greek word (*authenteō*) discovered during Paul's time, the earliest in a book called *Methodus mystica* involving astrology and the zodiac. An unborn Greek child's future social status was "described as one of seven possibilities, depending on the position of the planet Hermes—that is, Mercury—relative to the zodiac and the other planets at the time of the inquiry."[14] Mercury, in position seven (the furthest away), indicates one who is superior (*authenteō – an authority*) to other workers in his occupation and yet earns nothing. In other words, this person surpasses the other tradesmen in skill, yet is not paid for his work, suggesting a servant. Think along the lines of a natural born servant leader.

The fact that Paul raises the issue, and uses such a specific and rare word for authority, would seem to indicate that at least one woman in the early church may have been like "one who is superior [in skill]" mentioned above, but, given the massive culture shock the Gospel was creating, Paul deemed it necessary—at that moment in time—for tradition to trump ability. Furthermore, if a woman (or anyone for that matter) was assuming unbestowed authority, Paul's directive to submit would seem all the more necessary—both then and now.

Paul was not a man whose words were chosen lightly. In fact, seven of the eight occurrences in the New Testament in which wives are directed—directed, not forced—to submit to their husbands are in Paul's letters to the early churches. Knowing how deeply he engaged women in the early church, it is impossible to conclude that Paul was anti-women. More likely what we are seeing in these "loaded verses" is evidence of The Great Submission: the whole church being asked, in different ways, to submit to one another out of reverence to Christ.

Let's return for a moment to the Little League field, where the coach begins to teach the kids that to win games they must play as a team. Playing as a team means that no individual performance takes priority over the whole. Now, many sports may pay lip service to this idea, but no other sport has the language of submission built into it. What is a sacrifice bunt if not a submission of the ego of a given batter to the larger goal of the team? What is an RBI if not a formal way of recognizing the contribution of the one who will never get the personal rush of crossing home plate? Is it an easy lesson to learn?

Hardly. Young baseball players need to be taught to high five the teammate who makes his way back to the dugout after an out that advances a runner. Outs intuitively feel like losses. Submitting intuitively feels like giving something up—because it is. Submission is willingly giving up your immediate need, want, and preference out of love for someone or something other. As Wm. Paul Young says in the *New York Times* Bestseller *The Shack*, "Submission is not about authority and it is not obedience; it is all about relationships of love and respect."

These three words—*submission, obedience, authority*—are part of a common family of loaded ideas, particularly about authority; who gets it, and what our obligations are to yield to it. There is always much to be learned by noting the first use of a word in Scripture, and *authority* is no exception. "They should collect all the food of these good years that are coming and store up the grain under the **authority** of Pharaoh, to be kept in the cities for food" (Genesis 41:35). Notice that it is not Pharaoh, the authority, who is speaking, but Joseph, a young man left for dead by his own brothers, imprisoned for years, and now called in to interpret the Pharaoh's dreams. In this passage, it is Joseph who is viewed as the authority, and soon, that will become official:

> Then Pharaoh said to Joseph, "Since God has made all this known to you, there is no one so discerning and wise as

you. You shall be in charge of my
palace, and all my people are to **submit**
to your orders. Only with respect to the
throne will I be greater than you"
(Genesis 41:39-49 NRSV).

Pharaoh, the absolute human authority, humbles
himself before the lowly man with the gift of interpreting
dreams and elevates him above all others, an act that will
end up saving many nations. Here we have a biblical
example of how authority is appropriately used, how all
authority ultimately comes from God, and why we are to
treat authority with due reverence. A similar reversal of
authority through submission occurs in Matthew 3:13:

Then Jesus came from Galilee to the
Jordan to John, to be baptized by
him. John would have prevented him,
saying, "I need to be baptized by you,
and do you come to me?" But Jesus
answered him, "Let it be so now, for
thus it is fitting for us to fulfill all
righteousness." Then he consented.

As the 21st–century world of business tries to
define the ideal model for leadership they find
themselves—unwittingly—leaning towards an almost
"biblical" ideal. Leaders by definition *have* authority, but
are most successful when they use it to build consensus
and empower the team. If you have been in any kind of

corporate culture over the past few decades you may have witnessed the growing shift from a purely hierarchal model to a flatter, more collaborative, organizational structure. This modern "re-org" can help us understand the seismic reversal in how men and women, slave and free, Jew and Gentile, were being asked to relate to one another according to Jesus—and just how difficult it was.

Paul's instructions tended to come in pairs. Consider this loaded phrase: "For the wife does not have authority over her own body, but the husband does." Many fail to include in their reading and teaching of this verse the second half of the sentence. "**Likewise**, the husband does not have authority over his own body, but the wife does" (1 Corinthians 7:4). Given the culture of the ancient world, the most startling thing about this section seems to be the set-up: "The husband should give to his wife her conjugal rights, and likewise the wife to her husband." [15] Whose rights are mentioned first? The wife's. Whether her "conjugal rights" mean her own good pleasure, her own need to feel wanted by her husband, or her right to get pregnant and fulfill her desire for children, the fact that Paul speaks of her conjugal rights *at all*, let alone first, was game-changing. In fact, Paul appears to be the first writer from the Greco-Roman world to suggest that sexual pleasure could be mutual. And that both sexes are saved from the slippery slope of lust and distraction by this mutual covenant of sexual relations that binds them.[16]

We see the same pairings in nearly identical passages in Colossians 3:18 and Ephesians 5:21-24—wives submit to husbands; husbands care for wives with the sacrificial love of Christ. In 1 Peter, we hear this loaded phrase again, "wives, in the same way, submit yourselves to your husbands," but now it's the wives that are being told that *they* are to demonstrate the sacrificial love of Christ. Why? "So that, if any of them [husbands] do not believe the word, they may be won over without words by the behavior of their wives" (1 Peter 3:1). In other words, her submission is a tool which she willingly uses to demonstrate to a non-believing husband the way Christian love works. One can't help but think of the classic scene in the movie *My Big, Fat, Greek Wedding*, when the matriarch in the very patriarchal Greek family explains to her 1st-generation American daughter, "the man is the head, but the woman is the neck. And she can turn the head any way she wants."

Today, problems arise when church people and persecutors alike edit these verses for their own purposes. Against a backdrop of "I am woman hear me roar," it is easy to see how the culture would turn the idea of submission into a proof point that the church wants to hold women back. Yanked out of context, "wives submit to your husbands," is textbook sound bite material. At the same time, many churches—likely, too many—allow their male members to use these verses to control rather than to uplift their wives. This is an abuse of Scripture. A proper use will always consider context. You can't pull a few words out of a verse to achieve your own goals. And you can't pull a teaching out of historical context and hold it up to ideals of modern culture. Scholars Gordon Fee and Douglas Stuart assert, "A text cannot mean what it never could have meant to its author or his or her readers."[17] The Gospel that opened wide the gates of grace to women, slaves, and every marginalized soul on earth did not—and never could—seek to oppress them.

As we've seen throughout this book, words carry baggage and baggage keeps us from the truth. It also allows an easy "in" for the Enemy. "What's that?" Satan says. "Women don't want to submit to God or their husbands? Ha, I'm going to have a field day with this one." So it is that in 2011 we see an erotic novel arise from the pen of a middle-aged woman celebrating the idea of utter and complete sexual submission to the point of degradation and loss of free will. It began as a self-published effort, the kind that sells—if the author is lucky—about 100 books. But this one struck a chord, the disordered chord of submission. Women of every age and strata began passing it around like some new teaching on salvation. A major publisher got wind of it and helped catapult to the top of the charts a story that's unique selling point is its unabashed scenes of bondage/disciple, dominance/submission, and sadism/masochism.

Fifty Shades of Grey has sold over 100 million copies and has been translated into 52 languages. Woman around the globe, even as they protest the idea of submitting to the man in the bed beside them, are devouring the salacious story of a young college girl and a wealthy, attractive business man, whose name is, not coincidentally, Christian. Early on she asks him to explain the terms of their relationship:

> "So you'll get your kicks by exerting your
> will over me."
> "It's about gaining your trust and your
> respect, so you'll let me exert my will over
> you. I will gain a great deal of pleasure,
> joy, even in your submission. The more
> you submit, the greater my joy—it's a
> very simple equation."
> "Okay, and what do I get out of this?"
> He shrugs and looks almost apologetic.
> "Me," he says simply.

Paul told us this is how it would happen when we continually reject God in favor of our own delicious idols: "Therefore God gave them up in the lusts of their hearts to impurity, to the dishonoring of their bodies among themselves, because they exchanged the truth about God for a lie and worshiped and served the creature rather than the Creator, who is blessed forever!" (Romans 1:24-25).

There is no such thing as a life without submission. Whether in our roles as parents, spouses, neighbors, workers, church members, or friends, we are always submitting to something. The choice is ours. Jesus makes it pretty easy: "Take my yoke upon you, and learn from me, for I am gentle and lowly in heart, and you will find rest for your souls. For my yoke is easy, and my burden is light" (Matthew 11: 29-30).

SUBMIT
UNLOADED

- Submission is always an act of free will.

- We all submit to someone or something—all the time.

- Men and women are asked to submit to *each other* out of love.

- Jesus promises His yoke is easy and His burden light.

Study Questions
SUBMIT

1. Can you think of a time you have submitted to someone? Do you think people connect the word *submit* to everyday actions and life?

2. According to page 108, what are the top three *Oxford English Dictionary* definitions of submit? What is the important point made about these definitions?

3. READ Genesis 16:1-9. This is the first time that the original Hebrew is translated to the word submit in English. What are some of the remarkable features about this story? On pages 109-111 what do the authors assert are some notable features?

4. READ Ephesians 5:19-31. *Loaded Words* teaches that there was simply no model for this kind of marriage relationship. Why? What was so radical about these concepts? Does the information on pages 112-113 give you some insight?

5. Scripture shows us again and again that women were Paul's fellow workers. So why would Paul assert the need for submission? On pages 115-116 we read what was going on in Ephesus at the time Paul wrote his first letter to Timothy. What does this say?

6. READ Genesis 41:39-49 and Matthew 3:13-15. Thinking about the definition of Paul's unusual word for authority explained on pages 117-118, how do you think these verses explain the concept of "servant leadership"? How is this an act of submission?

7. On page 119 the authors write: Submission is _____ your _____ need, want, and preference _____ for someone or something _____ than yourself. How does the Little League example help you translate this concept?

Chapter 9

CHURCH

About life in the church no truer words were ever spoken: "Church would be great if it weren't for the people." People outside the church see only the ugly and the newsworthy, or, even more commonly, no people at all—just a hulking, impersonal entity. People inside the church tend to see other's sins more readily than their own—particularly those of the church down the street that adheres to a different interpretation of doctrine. And so it is that we move from the Big "C" to the Little "c" church as if they were interchangeable, every action taken in its name archived and hurled anew for all eternity. Like Facebook posts that can never be deleted, the Church must carry with it its history of weakness and vainglory and violence and shame. And every year, when some local church or avowed "Christian" does or says some wretched or unfathomable thing, we, the big "C" Church—looming like a cold, Medieval monolith—must take on its baggage. This, while social media metastasizes the impression so that one soul's misdeed in a single town becomes the face of each and every church in America.

Is this a fair picture of life in the neighborhood church? No. But before we can talk about joy and love and hope and belonging and the living God at work in our midst, we must own the truth that the world so often sees: that The Church—your church, my church—is filled with embarrassing uncles, gossipy aunts, finger-wagging pundits, lonely leeches, demanding donors, and the real and tragically insidious work of the enemy seeking to dismantle it from within. Oh, yes, and you. And me. As Charles Spurgeon notes, "the day we find the perfect church, it becomes imperfect the moment we join it."

The first "churches" were not churches at all, but "gatherings" in the desert, where God's people travelled far and wide to assemble as one to hear His Word. Think Coachella, the California rockfest that has grown to attract over a quarter million indie music lovers to an obscure dot of desert in the tumbleweed town of Indio. The people of Israel flocked to the "tent of meeting" with the same zeal with which true music fans first came to the Coachella Music Festival. Now, in its 15th year, Coachella is no longer so pure in heart. The people are no longer content to stand in the desert and listen: they need air conditioned party rooms, gourmet snacks, VIP seating, and, for those whose time is truly more valuable than the riffraff's, a private plane to fly them in over the congested, communal highway.

The first assemblies of the nomadic people of God were intended to be informal affairs, with no more permanence than a few tent poles. It seems that God preferred it that way. When David decided he wanted to build a house for God, God sent a prophet to correct him. "I have not lived in a house since the day I brought up the people of Israel from Egypt to this day, but I have been moving about in a tent and a tabernacle[1]" (2 Samuel 7:6 NRSV). From the beginning, God seemed reluctant to being "caged in" by structures. He knew what wood and stone and the selection of adornments can do to men and women; how easily sin can enter into the process. How easily the weighty permanence of an edifice can confuse people about the true power and spirit of God—whom "even heaven and the highest heaven cannot contain"[2]— or lead them to take for granted that He will always be found there. About this God is exceedingly clear: no amount of stained glass and good order can assure that He will continue to dwell in a house that has been overtaken by a superficial faith.[3] This is the bottom line on why the biblical meaning of *church* can never be a building: buildings can't believe.

One of the grave misdeeds of the historical Church was allowing the word *church* to be used in translation in the first place. The word "church" didn't enter the English lexicon until the 12th century, with the

primary definition being "a building for worship."[4] Suddenly, as new translations were being created, the powers that be appear to have intentionally chosen this word—one that supported buildings and the clergy that filled them—so as to ensure their continued financial support and unquestionable authority.[5] The most pivotal of these "translations" was the substitution in Matthew 16:18, "Upon this rock, I will build my *church*." The trouble is Jesus never said that. He never would have said that. He wouldn't even have said *synagogue*.[6] Because he was never talking about a building; he was talking about a people, **the people** who had been called out by God to gather together as one in the Holy Spirit. They were intended to be bound, not by a building, but by the sacrificial love of Christ who promised to be with them wherever two or more were gathered.

The word Jesus chose to express that idea was *ekklesia*, a Greek word we see in common use as far back as the 5th century BC.[7] At that time it was designated not as a religious word, but a civic one. It indicated an assembly of "all competent citizens" for the purposes of discussing matters of the common good. The gatherings opened with prayers and sacrifices to the officially recognized "gods of the city." Each citizen was entitled to speak and to propose matters for discussion. All decisions were made by majority rule. The ancient Greeks did not include women or slaves in their democratic process, but Jesus did. And although he does not use *ekklesia* in exactly the same way, he is likely telling us something

about equality and democracy within the church body—
what Martin Luther considered, "the priesthood of all
believers." As John Updike writes about the church[8];
"surely in all democracy there is nothing like it....Only in
church and at the polls are we actually given our
supposed value, the soul-unit of one, with its noumenal[1]
arithmetic of equality; one equals one."

Jesus only uses the word *ekklesia* two times, but
still he is clear about how we are to be together as his
community of believers.[9] "My mother and my brothers
are those who hear the word of God and do it" (Luke
8:21). Therefore, we are to be a new family, rooted in
willing obedience to Him, students of his Word and
servants to all. And together, we are to be "the light of the
world." Easier said than done. Perhaps this is why Jesus
uses the word *ekklesia* in these two specific—and
interrelated—instances. The first, to indicate how he will
build His assembly of believers ("On this rock..."), and
the second—on which the first ultimately hinges—in a
painfully simple instruction about how we are to resolve
conflict as brothers and sisters:

> If your brother sins against you, go and
> tell him his fault, between you and him
> alone. If he listens to you, you have
> gained your brother. But if he does not

---

[1] From the Greek nous, it is "the center of the human person, where mind
and matter meet most profoundly, and where the human person is mystically
united to others and to God." Scott Cairns in *Endless Life: Poems of the
Mystics.*

listen, take one or two others along with you, that every charge may be established by the evidence of two or three witnesses. If he refuses to listen to them, tell it to the church. And if he refuses to listen even to the church, let him be to you as a Gentile and a tax collector (Matthew 18:15-17).

This sounds like a perfectly lovely idea. We may spend many years in the *ekklesia* even believing that this is the standard for reconciliation that we use. But if you've been around the church for a while, you have no doubt experienced a more typical pattern of behavior. It goes something like this:

If your brother sins against you, go find someone to tell so you can get sympathy. If they agree that you have been sinned against, tell some more people—in secret of course—so that the sympathy can build to something like outrage. After you have spoken to several people you are free to state the fact that "everyone thinks so." If the pastor or the elders or the church council or anyone in charge doesn't do something to fix it, and make it clear to everyone that you were right and the other person was wrong, then you should

start speaking badly about the leaders,
too. Or maybe, since you seem to be the
only one trying to live by true scriptural
beliefs, leave the church and go find one
where they solve problems the way
Jesus said to.

Although the Gospels say surprisingly little about
"the church," the triune God knows there is much to be
said. He assigns the heavy lifting to Paul in his epistles—
where 62 of the 114 references to *ekklesia* are found—
and to Luke, in the book of Acts, where the miracles and
movement of the early church are testified to. Beginning
with Paul, and especially in 1 Corinthians 11-13, we see
that he speaks nothing about worship ministries or church
growth programs, but of how men and woman are to play
their parts, how the rich and the poor are to interact in a
way that makes them true and equal brothers, and how
those of different gifts and callings are to live out their
roles with the same level of value and respect. Despite all
our delusions of progress, these are the very things we in
the church still butt heads over today.

Unfortunately, the one sin Paul didn't directly
address is people coming and going each Sunday as if
they are visitors at a museum and not members of the
household of God. In other words, apathy. Our societal
apathy was first reported widely in *Bowling Alone*, a title
which came from Robert Putnam's research showing that,
although the popularity of bowling in the 21st century had

increased greatly, the participation in bowling leagues had dropped by 73%.[10] The truth of these numbers is felt far and wide in an era where cynicism and hubris have replaced conviction, thoughtfulness, and earnestness as the mark of a cultivated worldview. For the local church this means that most newcomers who enter their sanctuaries today—if they're lucky enough to attract them at all—will be a product of the culture at large; namely, apathetic participants. Without a church culture that supports an ever-deepening faith life—and sometimes even with one—these newcomers will not likely choose to move beyond milk "to solid food." This is not merely a problem of the young or the newly seeking: many lifelong church members come and go each Sunday morning with little thought of how they might be called to grow, learn, or serve more deeply.

So, for the apathetic and disengaged among us St. Paul speaks these words of truth: you don't get to be a Christian all by yourself. And you don't get to just take, take, take. Part and parcel of the Christian life is participating in the life of the Body, the assembly, the *ekklesia*, which is characterized by mutual love, upbuilding, unity, and service. To express this notion more deeply, Paul uses a different Greek word: *koinonia.* The word is translated as "fellowship," but it is not to be confused with something as secular as the camaraderie of an affinity group—knitters, bikers, surfers, chess-players, Bach-lovers, Nascar fanatics, vegans—but of something wholly new: what Luke sees as a unity, unanimity, and interdependence formed and sustained by the Holy Spirit—all hands together, and all eyes on God, with Christ at the center, the lifeblood, the glue.

The *ekklesia* is not a club or a happening or a fad. It is the means by which Jesus Christ lives and dwells among his people for all time, in all places, in all generations, calling this man, this teen, this family, together as one to live out the *koinonia* of believers.[11] *You* have been called here, by name, to this very church, and here you shall serve this Body and the Kingdom of God. Your being at this church at this moment in time is not random. Nor is it any different than the moment when God commanded His people to leave Egypt. Here is where He first uses the word "congregation."[12] It is as if He is telling them—and us—you are now a formed group, named as such by the Lord. Stay together.

Stay together. Love one another—even when people behave badly. Help one another—even when they're lazy. Encourage one another—even when you're feeling cynical and resistant. Recognize each other's gifts—even if you wish you had a different one. Trust one another—even if, inevitably, you'll be betrayed. Forgive one another—because in the end, you can't detach yourself from the *ekklesia* to which God has called you any more than you can truly disconnect from your own family, or your own history. Hopping around. Bowing out. None of this will save you. Because there is no perfect church, and no saving grace but Christ's. And no way of using the spiritual gifts you've been given without a table to bring them to.

For many who've grown up in the church, it's no doubt frustrating to see visitors failing to join, or regular members failing to study or grow in the knowledge of Scripture or their faith. About this, Martin Luther minces no words:

> Are we not the most marvelous fellows, therefore, who allow ourselves to imagine that, after reading and hearing it once, we know everything and need not read and study it anymore? We think we can learn in an hour what God himself cannot finish teaching, though he were to teach it from the beginning of the world until the end. All the prophets and all the saints have had to learn it, but they have always remained its pupils, and they must continue to do so.[13]

This seems like a lot to ask of an over-booked modern American just trying to squeeze a little church into his week, but Luther makes sure to offer an incentive: "If they show such diligence, then I promise them—and their experience will bear me out—that they will gain much fruit and God will make excellent people out of them."[14]

For those of us who have made our way to solid

food through time and prayer and study, it is up to us—in the spirit of *koinonia*—to stir in the complacent follower a true desire to know God's word. Maybe—just maybe— if we can be courageous and faithful in this, all may grow in the knowledge of Christ, and in doing so, "let your light shine before others, so that they may see your good works and give glory to your Father who is in heaven" (Matthew 5:16).

To the outside world, The Church remains a baffling and often unwelcoming place. But for those who've dared to follow the whisper of the Spirit inside the walls where Christ's people gather now in worship, it is, and continually becomes, "the community of people in which and through which the Spirit of God is working."[15] This might be welcome news to those who feel the inequality of the world is overwhelming, that the noise of the world is inescapable, that the lies of the world are too thick to overcome. Let us, the Church, in all that we say and do be ever mindful of them, that they, too, may one day feel the psalmist's words leaping from their own hearts, "I rejoiced with those who said to me, let us go to the house of the Lord!" (Psalm 122:1 NIV).

CHURCH
UNLOADED

- There is no such thing as a perfect church.

- All churches, like families, are filled with flawed characters.

- The meaning of *church* is the gathering and not the walls.

- We are meant to live, love, learn, suffer, and grow in the community we call *church*.

Study Questions
CHURCH

1. What are some of the ways the culture has come
    to think of "the church."

2. READ 2 Samuel 7:1-6. What does this tell you
    about God's definition of "church"? Does the
    illustration about Coachella on pages 130-131
    help? Can you think of other such gatherings –
    secular or sacred?

3. According to the authors, on pages 131-132, when
    was the English word church first used to translate
    the ancient Greek? How does this compare to
    definition of "church" from the 2 Samuel passage
    you just read in question 2.

4. What Greek word, do we learn on pages 132-133,
    did Jesus use that we have translated to "church?"
    What is the important difference between the
    modern understanding and the original definition?

5. READ Matthew 16:18. Why is translating this
    word to *church* instead of "gathering" so
    problematic?

6. According to pages 135, what word did Luke and
    Paul use that we have translated to *church* in
    English? What "heavy-lifting" did Paul and Luke
    do?

7. Rather than being contained within the walls of a
    building, we read on pages 136-137, Paul
    suggests that believers are connected in another
    way. He uses two concepts: *koinonia* and body of
    believers. What do these concepts tell us?

Chapter 10

JUDGMENT

"I have a dream that my four little children will one day live in a nation where they will not be judged by the color of their skin but by the content of their character."[1] In 1963, when these indelible words were spoken, the vast majority of Americans did not nod and smile and claim this truth as their own. "I Have a Dream" was a righteous and Scripture-inspired judgment against racism, a judgment that ultimately cost Martin Luther King, Jr. his life. But at the heart of his message was a truth more universal than the relations between black and white in 20th-century America. His words were the deepest of all human cries across all time and culture. **Justice**! Not the elimination of judgment, but the assurance that judgments will be made fairly and with respect to the character of each man, woman, and child. Fifty-plus years later, *Time Magazine* claimed that, "with a single phrase, Martin Luther King, Jr. joined Jefferson and Lincoln in the ranks of men who've shaped modern America." And all three of them joined the psalmist who wrote:

> Arise, O Lord, in your anger;
> lift yourself up against the fury of my enemies;
> awake for me; you have appointed a judgment.
> Let the assembly of the peoples be gathered
> about you; over it return on high.
> The Lord judges the peoples;
> judge me, O Lord, according to my righteousness
> and according to the integrity that is in me.
> Oh, let the evil of the wicked come to an end,
> and may you establish the righteous—
> you who test the minds and hearts
> O righteous God! (Psalm 7:6-9).

When we think about the word *judgment*, this is what we must remember: judgment is the vehicle by which justice is meted out. Our challenges with the word *judgment* today come not from the existence of—or necessity for—judgment in the world, but from the heart and spirit with which judgmental actions are taken.

The Old Testament was a different story. The people of Israel understood that justice was dispensed, as needed, to restore peace in a community, tribe or family.[2] They recognized that those in positions of making decisions about right and wrong were instruments of God and had been tasked with the great responsibility of "setting things to rights." You would never hear someone in the ancient world shout, "stop being so judgmental!" Judgment, they knew, supported the most foundational and absolute principle of all Old Testament law: **equity**.[3] This call to be equitable was greater than the rights of nations or individuals, and lies at the heart of the Jewish ideal of *tikkun olam*, or, the healing of the world.

Curiously, the people who were called on to *judge* (*šāpaṭ*) were not primarily "judges" in the formal, judicial sense. In fact, in the book of Judges, we see that God uses a variety of people—a sword-fighter, a female prophetess, an uncertain fleece-tester, a beautifully-haired man with supernatural strength—in the role of judge. When we look more closely at the Hebrew root for the word that is translated as judge—*šōperîm*—we find that it is essentially synonymous with *deliverer*.[4] In the language of God, then, we see that making decisions about right and wrong, and taking action on those decisions—in other words, *judging*—is a critical component of saving people.

When an addict or an obese person is told they must change the way they live because they are not only killing themselves they are hurting the people they love, this is a judgment passed to save a life. We even have a name for it: tough love. When there is oppression in a third world country and the voices of equitable treatment worldwide rise up and say **enough!,** these are the sounds of life-saving judgment. These voices—liberal and conservative, Christian and secular—unite in their belief that women, children, or nations should not be treated in a way that goes against their natural-born rights—what many call God-given rights. And those rights can only be protected, defended—and those people saved—when judgment is first passed.

We tend not to think of it in this way when we speak of judgment in the culture today. Take a look at the average Twitter feed and you'll find such common tweets as: *Why are people so judgmental?/ Stop being so judgmental about everyone else's life and worry about your own/* I *can tell judgmental people just by looking at them/ "Christians" are the most judgmental people on earth.* What is interesting is that no one ever seems to tweet *Why is God so judgmental?* Their beef is with people, and specifically, with people claiming to judge them in the name of God. This is the pain point between the church and the culture. How *we* represent the judgment of God to others.

On the other hand, our contemporary culture seems to have no problem with judgment in the name of riches, glory, or snark. In fact, our willingness to participate—even celebrate—the process of judging is a multi-billion dollar industry. We have judges on *American Idol* and *The X-Factor* whom we empower to discern our giftedness for entertainment. We have shows such as *The Real World* and *Wife Swap* that allow the viewers to judge the behavior of regular people making ordinary day-to-day decisions about how to manage their lives. We have *Toddlers in Tiaras*, which allow us to judge the moms even as the pageant judges judge the kids. And, in a weekly Greek drama of man's pitiful efforts to please a vengeful god-figure, we have *The Apprentice*, and, the aptly named, *Hell's Kitchen*.

Entertainment aside, no person who has ever lived in or attempted to raise a family can claim to have transcended the human cycle of behavior in which judgment plays a part. From the moment we can discern a milky breast within our reach, we have a sense of what we're entitled to. Faced with delay or rejection, we summon the primal cry of **No Fair!** As we grow, we develop a highly-tuned sensitivity to whether or not our slice of cake or length of "turn" is wholly equitable—this is a child's judgment about fairness. A good part of the parenting process, then, is teaching that there are factors beyond a child's own desires that must be considered in the "big picture" of equity. No parent or child accomplishes this task perfectly. It is a lifelong challenge for all people, this act of learning to think a little less of our own needs and desires, and consider the larger needs of the family, community, or world.

John 3:30 sums it up nicely: "He must increase, but I must decrease."

What?!! Why should Jesus get more than me?! Why not just cut him right out of the picture—then we

can have the whole cake ourselves, right? Certainly that
seems like a reasonable point of view for those who have
yet to hear the Gospel—or Jesus's views on judgment. He
likes to keep it simple. "Judge not, that you be not
judged" (Matthew 7:1). There we have it. The Golden
Rule. The universal standard for equity across all time
and culture. Just in case we missed the point, Jesus
unpacks it for us even more:

> For with the judgment you pronounce
> you will be judged, and with the
> measure you use it will be measured to
> you. Why do you see the speck that is in
> your brother's eye, but do not notice the
> log that is in your own eye? Or how can
> you say to your brother, 'Let me take the
> speck out of your eye,' when there is the
> log in your own eye? You hypocrite,
> first take the log out of your own eye,
> and then you will see clearly to take the
> speck out of your brother's eye (Matthew
> 7:2-5).

As Christians, then, we are asked first to judge
ourselves, then to clean up our own acts, and, if we
manage to do that—a life's work to be sure—then, and
only then, are we asked to help a neighbor "remove" his
sin. The task Jesus sets before us is humbling to say the
least: assume that our own sin is infinitely larger than
whatever we imagine we see in someone else. Now

maybe it is and maybe it isn't. We can't tell for sure. But God can. Which is why we are instructed to judge painstakingly, behaving towards others with the sure knowledge that, on the last day—in the ultimate, cosmic act of equity—"Christ will judge the secret thoughts of all" (Romans 2:16 NRSV).

Isn't that the reassurance that we all seek? Isn't that the standard of fairness to which Martin Luther King referred? Yes. But. If we're honest, what we also want is to be able to look back and say, "See, we were right, and you were wrong." All of us. Christians and atheists and everyone in between. This is the darkness in the heart of man, and on this, we will all be judged.

We try to get around this ultimate judgment by throwing out all the rules, and demonizing anyone who claims there is an absolute standard of right and wrong. The great irony is that this does not make us freer, but rather, more enslaved. Even a child can see it. Consider the hit song from the movie, *Frozen*. In 2014, "Let it Go," was the *de facto* anthem of tween girls. And plenty of adults sang along with them the words, "no right, no wrong, no rules for me. I'm free." It is safe to say that these lines reflect the spirit of our contemporary culture, an era that echoes the climate found in Judges where: "everyone did what was right in his own eyes" (Judges 21:25).

But let's look at what's going on with the popularity of this song a little more closely. These tween girls are not bucking the pressures put on them by God, but by the culture, a culture that tells them they must have perfect bodies, perfect hair, perfect grades, perfect careers, and a secret command of how to please a boy sexually, even as they have a perfect command of birth control so they don't end up with anything less than a perfect husband. These are the pressures—the undeniable judgments—that lead girls to shout with joy these lyrics: "Let it go, let it go. And I'll rise like the break of dawn. Let it go, let it go. That perfect girl is gone."

When we throw out Godly judgment, we get in its stead the judgment of man, which—lacking omniscience or a commitment to equity—will always skew to the obvious, earthly victors: being perfect and being right. In a culture that worships tolerance, the need to be right should be obsolete. Instead, we live in a sound-bite media culture that spews a 24/7 stream of anger and insults and judgments, where daily, people of all beliefs and practices—and no beliefs and practices—try to demean or eviscerate the other, and people get rich letting them doing it. Paul sums in up nicely with this patchwork of Scripture—Psalms, Proverbs, Prophets—all underscoring the universality of God's judgment:

As it is written:

"None is righteous, no, not one;
no one understands;

no one seeks for God.
All have turned aside; together they
have become worthless;
no one does good,
not even one."
"Their throat is an open grave;
they use their tongues to deceive."
"The venom of asps is under their lips."
"Their mouth is full of curses and bitterness."
"Their feet are swift to shed blood;
in their paths are ruin and misery,
and the way of peace they have not known."
"There is no fear of God before their eyes"
(Romans 3:10-18).

We will all be judged. We are all wrong. But Christians are more wrong than others because we have heard Jesus's words and not taken them to heart. In fact, we are often more like Pharisees than servants:

> Woe to you, scribes and Pharisees, hypocrites! For you tithe mint and dill and cumin, and have neglected the weightier matters of the law: justice and mercy and faithfulness. These you ought to have done, without neglecting the others. You blind guides, *straining out* a gnat and swallowing a camel! (Matthew 23:23-24 *emphasis ours*).

Here we see the Greek word for *judge* (*krisis*) that means justice, or perhaps more clearly, the administration of fairness. Fairness is always at the heart of judgment. In the last line the judge-root (*krima*) is brought to life through the images of the day. *Krima,* frequently used by Homer and other classical Greek writers, incorporates the idea of "sifting."[5] In a modern home kitchen, a baker might use a sifter to make sure that the hard lumps of powdered sugar don't get through, which would impact the quality of the whole cake. In this scenario, the lumps are judged "bad." But often times, the thing that is kept on the top of the sifter is desirable: consider sifting for gold or the modern healing techniques made possible by blood fractionation—sifting for platelets, plasma, and component parts. Another everyday equivalent of this sifting might be "assessment," a practice that has become central to business and educational practices. We are forever deciding if this technique or that was effective, and making judgment calls about whether to retain it or "let it go".

The bottom line is this: throughout all our daily lives there are needs to define, to separate, to distinguish, and to make decisions. What is required of us as believers is that we "judge not by appearances, but with right judgment."[6] Jesus gives this warning to the religious leaders of the day when they were demonstrating, once again, that they cared more about the Law than about people.[7] In fact, every verse in which Jesus teaches how one man is to judge another can be summed up with this simple refrain: **care more about your neighbor than about being right.**

In every era, there are political and/or social issues that sorely test this standard. Ours is no exception. It is impossible to know how God is at work in light of current issues, only that He *is* at work. Perhaps this is easier if we trust not only the ancient wisdom of Scripture but also the empirical wisdom of our own lives revealing that time brings new perspective. It would have been impossible to imagine in 1963, for example, that Martin Luther King was setting into motion a movement that would lead us to elect Barak Obama as president in 2008.

When we recognize that we are not always able to see the "big picture" from ground zero of our daily cultural conflicts, it makes it easier to understand why God alone will judge our actions. God alone—Father, Son, and Holy Spirit—is the only one who can see every single angle, every intention, every repentant heart, and consider those in the light of His ultimate purpose. And He shows us time and again that these things are always cyclical. All of Scripture is, in fact, little more than a recycling logo of Sin>Repentance>Forgiveness, with judgment as the force of motion.

In the book of Judges, there is a well-established cycle that repeats in each of the Judge narratives: 1) Israel does what is evil in the eyes of the Lord; 2) the Lord gives them over to the hands of the oppressors; 3) Israel serves the oppressor for X years, 4) Israel cries out to the Lord; 5) the Lord raises up a deliverer (i.e., a judge); 6) the spirit of the Lord is upon the deliverer; 7) the oppressor is subdued; 8) the land has "rest" for X years.[8] Now substitute, say, America for Israel, and false gods— money, power, fame, sex, self-righteousness—for "oppressors." It is impossible for us to know where we are in a given cycle. Impossible to discern, for example, when Pope Francis, in 2013, said stunningly, "Who am I to judge?" if we are entering a stage 2 or a stage 6. We can't know. But God can. Which is why He asks us to leave the whole thing in His more than capable hands.

But we're His instruments, aren't we? Absolutely. Of love and mercy, calibrating our judgments to those ends. Even when it's hard. Which it will be. Growth always is. Consider the story of Pastor Johnson Rethinasamy, a fifth-generation Indian Lutheran who came to New York City to get his PhD. He started playing the organ in a Lutheran church to pay his rent. The pastor there discovered that Rethinasamy was ordained and helped him get credentialed to serve in the U.S. He began a storefront ministry to Indians, Sri Lankans, Malaysians, Singaporeans, Pakistanis, and Bangladeshis. Through Word and sacrament, they quickly grew to a thriving all-South Asian congregation of 150 new immigrant Christians. Then, the call came. Would Pastor Johnson come to lead a small, stagnant, "old-German" Lutheran church in Queens?

Let's consider the role of judgment in this narrative. Faced with a church that was no longer thriving, the members of Immanuel Lutheran in Whitestone needed to sift their priorities and decide whether they cared more about retaining their German-Lutheran culture or about being "salt and light" in the neighborhood. They chose the latter. Now the ball was in Pastor Johnson's court. He needed to make a judgment about how God wanted him to serve, leading him to inform his new immigrant congregation that he would not take the call unless they came with him. Well, this did not go over well with the new conclave of South-Asian Christians. They liked their homogenous culture, maybe even more than they valued their pastor or the Word of God. Of the 150 members, only 50 agreed to follow.

Today, the multi-ethnic church calls itself a "Mosaic Ministry," offering services in six languages. They baptize babies and adults, and celebrate families coming to faith in Tamil, Mandarin, Cantonese, Hindi, Spanish and English. Their potlucks feature samosas and dumplings and lime Jell-O salad, and the kitchen is filled with German Lutherans and Sari-wrapped Lutherans and Chinese Lutherans and Puerto Rican Lutherans and Dominican Lutherans and a great outpouring of the Holy Spirit. Not all at Immanuel said yes to the new vision. But those who did have come to experience the Living God in a way that reveals the full mysteries of His love. And they've done it without compromise, judging

Orthodox teaching and the gift of the sacraments to be at
the heart of the Gospel.

This is the standard Christ gives us for "setting
things to rights." When we are feeling inclined to judge
let us begin with "the household of God," making sure
we are faithful servants of His means of grace. And
trusting with all our heart, soul, and mind that He is the
one who will come again to "*judge* both the living and
the dead."

Until then, our job is simply to love.

JUDGMENT
UNLOADED

- Judgment is the vehicle by which justice is meted out.

- When we reject God's judgment we become subject to man's.

- Jesus tells us to judge others the way we would want to be judged.

- Christian judgment requires caring more about your neighbor than about being right.

Study Questions
JUDGMENT

1. Why do people inside and outside the church dislike the word *judgment*?

2. According to the authors, on page 145, what was the foundational principle for Old Testament law? Who were the people responsible for meting out justice and what was the purpose?

3. Looking at typical comments, on page 146, what do you think is "the beef" between the church and the culture in terms of the word *judgment*?

4. READ Matthew 7:1-5. Why is this especially important for Christians to understand?

5. What do you think about this statement on page 149: If we're honest, what we also want is to be able to look back and say, "See, we were right, and you were wrong." All of us. Christians and atheists and believers of all kinds. This is the darkness in the heart of man, and on this, we will all be judged.

6. What do you think about the relationship between equity and judgment described throughout this chapter?

7. When we throw out Godly judgment, according to the authors on page 150, we get in its stead the judgment of man, which lacks omniscience or a commitment to equity. READ Romans 3:10-18. According to Paul what is missing from the judgment of man?

8. From page 153, what is the easiest way to sum up Jesus's guiding principle of how one man is to judge another?

Chapter 11

RELIGION

In our pluralistic, relativistic, anything goes and everything's equal culture, the pull-down menu that is *religion* is growing very long indeed. For Sufism, press 5. For Scientology, press 6. For atheism, press 7. The category has become so broad and inclusive that a standard definition is no longer possible. Sure, Merriam Webster will lead off with "a belief in a god or a group of gods," but right on its heels is "an interest, belief or activity that is very important to a person or group." Global cultural scholars Peter Mandaville and Paul James define *religion* as "a relatively-bounded system of beliefs, symbols and practices that addresses the nature of existence, and in which communion with others and Otherness is lived as if it both takes in and spiritually transcends socially-grounded ontologies of time, space, embodiment and knowing."[1] Does that clear it up for you?

Trickier still is the fact that the word *religion,* apparently, did not enter the Scriptures until the 13th-century,[2] when the Latin *religio* was used to capture the essence of James 1:26, "If any think they are religious, and do not bridle their tongues but deceive their hearts, their religion is worthless." Even the roots of the word *religio* are contested. There is evidence that the pagan philosopher Cicero first coined the term just before the birth of Christ by combining *re* (again) + *lego* (to choose or carefully consider). According to thoughtful scholars, Cicero used it to describe people who took matters of moral obligation, the Supreme Good, and the importance of gods seriously. The inclusion of the "re" is interesting, because it implies that what is to be considered is not new—either to the person, or in history—but rather already in existence.[3]

There is also strong support among modern scholars—including popular mythologist Joseph Campbell—that Augustine's first take on the origins of *religio* is the correct one: *re* (again) + *ligere* (to connect). In other words, to reconnect to God, something that would only be necessary if a connection once existed and was broken. But even Augustine in his own lifetime had a change of heart, deciding that the most inspired interpretation of the origin of the word *religion* was from the little known 4th century *theologian* Lactantius, who believed it came from the Latin *religare* (to bind). Lactantius asserted that we are bound to God by the bond of piety, an image that has particular potency in light of the Old Testament narrative of Abraham, who *bound* his son Isaac as a model of faithful conduct.[4] It is this definition—to rebind—that is favored by contemporary writers, but there is surely wisdom to be found in each of the possible roots: to reconsider, to reconnect, and to rebind.

As we know, there is no Latin in the original Scripture. Back then, there was no real need for a word like *religion* since every aspect of life in the ancient world was touched by the relationship of man to the supernatural or divine. As theologian George Lindbeck notes, it was "a kind of cultural and/or linguistic framework or medium that shape[d] the entirety of life and thought."[5] What then are the Hebrew words—and later, in the NT, the Greek words—that have been translated into English as *religion*? Well, not unlike Eskimos having dozens of word forms for *ice* and *snow*, the Jews had many word themes and variations on what we see simply translated into this single word, *religion*. There is, however, one primary Hebrew word root from which *religion* springs: *Hagag*.

What do you think *hagag* means? Obey? Repent? Revere? Nope. **Celebrate!**[6] And not just a polite nod to the day, but a feasting, dancing, reeling festival so joyful that it embodies the notion of "staggering" (*ḥāgā*) like a sailor being tossed on a ship by exuberant waves. These celebrations were their Holy Days, what we now call holidays. It is this *hagag* which is at the heart of *religion*.

There were three divinely ordained "pilgrim feasts," beginning with the Passover. Within this one instructive verse, we can see how *hagag* is unpacked. "This day shall be for you a **memorial day**, and you shall **keep** it as a feast to the LORD; throughout your generations, as a statute **forever**, you shall **keep** it as a **feast**" (Exodus 12:14). "To keep these holy days in celebration" (*hagag*) is **how** they were to remember forever. The stem *hag* is the feasting part, done in a spirit of gratitude for blessings, for freedom, for the abundance of food with which God has blessed the earth. In stark contrast to how the word is often heard and understood today, the reality of *religion* is a glorious, romping, communal shout: Thank You, God!

Let's take a moment to compare this divinely ordained **Memorial Day**, to our own American national holiday of the same name. In a 2000 Gallup poll, only 28% of Americans could rightly state that Memorial Day was a day of remembrance for those who had died fighting for our country. By 2014, this number was no doubt lower, as only 5% of people planned to attend a parade, participate in a memorial service, or visit a gravesite.[7] Sure, we pass around "We'll Never Forget" memes on Facebook—just as we do on 9/11—but those assertions are only necessary because we do, of course, forget. We go on with our lives, and bit by bit, what we **keep** and **hold** loses its luster. Sure, we still gather and feast and stagger but we're not sure why. Memorial Day is now a great day to buy a car or a flat screen TV or get a great deal on bulk burgers at the local mega-mart. It's a great day to eat too much and drink too much and get a start on your summer tan. We do our best to make the day feel special, but there's a hole where the meaning used to be, a hole we fill up with the most sacred expression our modern spirits can muster: shopping.

God knows we are inclined to want to forget. Which is why He spreads the remembrances throughout the year. Fifty days after the Passover is the divinely ordained Feast of First Fruits to celebrate the early crops to which the earth gives rise (Leviticus 23: 15-16, 21). And then in the fall, as the harvest comes to an end, the Feast of Ingathering, and the simultaneous Feast of Booths, a physical reenactment of the days when they lived in tents and not in "the land of milk and honey."[8] God ordained these Holy Days to help them—us— remember where we came from, that we could fall on hard times again, that tomorrow's crops are not guaranteed. To remember that there but for the grace of God go I:

> For there will never cease to be poor in
> the land. Therefore I command you,
> 'You shall open wide your hand to your
> brother, to the needy and to the poor, in
> your land' (Deuteronomy 15:11).

It seems there are a lot of things we've forgotten. Human nature being what it is, we don't like to be reminded that the good times might end, or give anyone else any credit for our good fortune. So we phase out the holy part of the holidays God gave us as a Celebration of Life (which we now save for our funerals) and blithely substitute one religion for another.   For consumerism, press 9.

Don't feel too badly. We're not the first. During the late 8th century BCE, a particularly peaceful and prosperous time, there seemed to be a widening gap between the rich and the poor, and a dimming memory of the spirit of God's statutes. And so it is that the prophet Amos is sent to deliver a message:

> I hate, I despise your feasts,
> and I take no delight in your
> solemn assemblies.
> Even though you offer me your burnt
> offerings and grain offerings,
> I will not accept them;
> and the peace offerings of your
> fattened animals,
> I will not look upon them.
> Take away from me the noise
> of your songs;
> to the melody of your harps I will
> not listen.
> But let justice roll down like waters,
> and righteousness like an ever-flowing
> stream (Amos 5:21-24).

Hypocrisy and false piety in the practice of religion is nothing new, but for now it's ours to contend with. How, then, are we to better hear and represent this original notion of *religion* to a wary culture? We can start by recognizing that those outside the church are not wary for nothing. We have often transmitted anger more readily than joy, and would be hard-pressed to find a secular soul (and perhaps more sadly, a Christian soul) who would guess that the root meaning of the words we have translated as *religion* is celebration.

The culture compounds the distance between us by coupling religion with the word "organized," as if to indicate some sort of corrupt, systematic plot. Have you ever noticed that the only other public endeavor to be labeled as "organized" in a pejorative way is The Mafia? But even in this accusatory use of the term "organized religion," the church has played a part. As far back as 1645, Scottish minister Robert Baillie decried the power and authority granted the "organized church" or "presbytery" versus the "inorganized or unpresbyterated,"[9] church. This tension between too much and too little structure, it seems, is just part of our human battle.

So much of these "religious" tensions come down to fear. Fear of death, of our own weakness, of losing control—or never having it. Fear of backing the wrong "horse" or backing the right one imperfectly. These are the fears of men, and they infiltrate the practice of each of our "religions"—from parenting, to health, to fiscal policy, to God. We want to be right, but we don't want to accept that being right begins with fear—not fear of men, but fear of the Lord, which, rightly understood, is "the beginning of wisdom" (Proverbs 9:10).

In both the Hebrew, *yārē'* and the Greek, *phobos*, this reverent awe we call fear is translated as *religion*.[10] And Paul uses the felt-truth of this fear to open wide the gates of Grace to all, meeting them at their own point of reverent longing, and connecting the dots to the God of all Creation:

> So Paul, standing in the midst of the Areopagus, said: "Men of Athens, I perceive that in every way you are very **religious**. For as I passed along and observed the objects of your worship, I found also an altar with this inscription, 'To the unknown god.' What therefore you worship as unknown, this I proclaim to you. The God who made the world and everything in it, being Lord of heaven and earth, does not live in temples made by man, nor is he served by human hands, as though he needed anything, since he himself gives to all mankind life and breath and everything. And he made from one man every nation of mankind to live on all the face of the earth, having determined allotted periods

and the boundaries of their dwelling
place, that they should seek God, and
perhaps feel their way toward him and
find him. Yet he is actually not far from
each one of us, for 'In him we live and
move and have our being'; as even some
of your own poets have said, 'For we are
indeed his offspring'" (Acts 17:22-28).

In the hands of God, fear is a beautiful thing. Trusting
this, let us return to the modern notion of *religion* as a
category with a menu of options, fearing nothing but the
wisdom of God.

Today it is widely accepted that the practice of
religion—any or none—is entirely a matter of personal
preference. This is based on the concept of truth being
relative, and therefore, each of us being free to determine
our own truth. This menu concept of religion is, of
course, only viable if there is no Absolute Truth, and that
the Only True Thing is an individual's Right To Choose
what they want to believe. Now, if it's true that there is
no Absolute Truth, then by all means, we should choose
our spiritual practices like we choose our cars or our
shoes or favorite pinot noir. The trouble is that the claim
that there is No Absolute Truth *is* an Absolute Truth
claim ... and so it goes in the world of "religion" and the
circular logic of truth: word games to keep one busy—
and distracted—to the end of time.

If that sort of thinking makes your head spin, try this: the menu approach to religion is akin to holding a police line-up without making the top priority identifying the actual criminal, but rather, making sure that the witnesses have the right to claim whichever scruffy fellow they please. Or, an image a little closer to home, it's like throwing an entire grade of high school seniors in an auditorium and telling them that the valedictorian can be anyone they want it to be; this, while the person who actually earned the highest GPA walks around stunned saying, "But, but, but...."

Ok, so let's line them up—the big world religions, and the indigenous native practices, and the great Eastern philosophies, and the new age, self-help creeds, and see if Christianity has any distinguishing characteristic other than the fact of its own claim to be the word of God. Christians believe this to be true, of course, but one can't hold onto that belief while looking at a menu or there wouldn't be any point in looking. So, here we are, perusing our options—Islam and Hinduism and Kaballah, Naturalism and Mormonism and Jehovah's Witnesses, Wicca and Christianity and Anthroposophy and Buddhism, to name just a few. It's a really long list and so diverse in intent and practice that a side-by-side comparison is all but impossible. Accept for one thing. (Two, if you count the part about it being the story of the world according to God). And that thing is this: the "religion" we call Christianity is the **only one** based not on earning salvation, or trying to figure out the meaning of life, or trying to find a way to be a better person, but on **giving thanks** for a wholly, unmerited gift that has already been given. Grace. This is why we worship. This is why we celebrate. This is why we forgive one another: because He first forgave us. Now, that doesn't prove it's true, but it does give us something to consider as we browse the menu.

Which brings us back to the word *religion*. In the wildly popular book *The Four Agreements*, based on the Toltec wisdom tradition, the first of the shaman's four guides to living is this: *Be impeccable with your word.* Notice that the word *impeccable* shares the Latin root *pecco*, which mean to err, go astray, or sin. The wisdom we find here harkens back to the idea of "my word is my bond." It also underscores the purpose of this book: to know what biblical words mean and to use them as they were intended. It is for this reason that the word *religion* cannot be used to speak to anything and everything one wants to believe. Because the word *religion* came through the people of God to reference the unique experiences of the Judeo-Christian faith as it moved from a season of promises to fulfillment.[11]

This is not a debatable point, but a fact.

Although there were as many spiritual practices— pagan, civic, ancestral, folkloric—in the ancient world as there are today, the word *religion* was planted in the very soil of the birthplace of Jesus Christ to underscore his promises—to reconnect and rebind all the peoples of the earth to the Living God. It was not intended to be used outside of His context. To do so—to call all belief systems *religion*—is, in effect, like calling all beverages water.

If Paul were with us today, he would likely say to those who gather to read *The Four Agreements*; or who sit in silence before a Buddha image longing to transcend suffering; or who stand atop the highest hill hoping to hear the truth of the universe; or who purchase Hindi statues out of a sincere desire to be about something older and wiser and broader and deeper than themselves but have no clue as to how to go about it; or who kiss the cheeks of their beloved children each night in reverent awe of their lives and the overwhelming beauty and terror of it all; or who thank God as they understand him for another day sober—to these Paul might say this:

> I see how extremely **[devout]** you are in every way. For as I went through the city and looked carefully at the objects of your worship, I found among them an altar with the inscription, 'To an unknown god.' What therefore you worship as unknown, this I proclaim to you: *He's not unknowable. He's right here. He has been all along. And will be until you draw your last breath, and even then, He'll be with you still, with*

both you and your children. His name is
Jesus.

This is the truth and experience that the word *religion* was created to express. When we misappropriate it, we are not being impeccable with our word. We are not being open or tolerant or non-judgmental. We are being inaccurate—maybe innocently, maybe not. Hard to say for sure but when we look at how we, the culture, have misappropriated the words *Christmas* and *Easter*, perhaps we can draw some parallel conclusions.

There is no need to highlight here what Christmas and Easter mean to most people in America today. One is certainly free to celebrate those days any way they like, and many devout Christians enjoy the more secular aspects of the occasion just as much as the next person. But one cannot say that Christmas is a **holiday** to celebrate *Santa Claus* or Easter is a **holiday** to celebrate a *basket-toting Bunny*. These words have meanings, and the meanings were intended to **hold** and **keep** the **holy** work of God through all time. A person may choose to deny this, and a culture may choose to force the OED to add entirely new and equally acceptable definitions, just as they did with *literally*. What they cannot do is change the original spirit and intent of the word.

So it is with *religion*: not one of many, but simply the one and only narrative of the people who feared God—as they understood and sought him—and their redemption throughout human history, **celebrated** then, now, and for all time. For those who long to *reconsider*, *reconnect* or *rebind* themselves to this ineffable *religious* Word, may we find it anew in the Gospel according to John:

> In the beginning was the Word, and the Word was with God, and the Word was God. He was in the beginning with God. All things were made through him, and without him was not any thing made that was made. In him was life, and the life was the light of men (John 1:1-5).

RELIGION
UNLOADED

- The Hebrew root word from which religion springs is *celebrate*.

- The "re" in religion reminds us that God is not new: He has been there all along.

- The word religion came through the people of God to reference the unique experiences of the Judeo-Christian faith.

- Calling all belief systems religions is like calling all beverages water.

Study Questions
RELIGION

1. How many "religions" can you name?

2. According to pages 162, when was the word religion first used and what were the three possible definitions?

3. We read on page 163, from the original Hebrew, what was the *primary definition* for the word we have translated to religion in English?

4. According to the authors, on pages 164, what was the purpose for these God ordained celebrations or "holy days?"

5. READ Amos 5:21-24. When you think about how our culture celebrates Memorial Day, Independence Day, Easter, Christmas or even Thanksgiving, how do we measure up against Amos' prophetic lament?

6. The menu concept of religion is based on the premise that there is no Absolute Truth. But, as

we read on pages 169, the claim that there is No
Absolute Truth *is* _____.

7. What is one important distinction, according to
    the authors on page 170-171, between the various
    "religions" and Christianity? How do you think
    this assertion would be received by people who
    don't believe in Jesus's gift of grace?

Chapter 12

CHRISTIAN

We begin with a love story that the world says can never be. "Tis but thy name that is my enemy," Juliet proclaims, launching the timeless Shakespearean passage that has led people around the globe to ponder this disruptive question "What's in a name?"[1] Is a name the essence of the thing itself, or merely a label for it? And if the label is attached to a person—as opposed to, say, a molecule or an algorithm—is its meaning and inference susceptible to the actions of the person who claims it as their own?

In the children's game Follow the Leader, being The Leader has always been the "name" to aspire to. But in one dark moment in history, a single German man took this name as his own—"der Fuhrer"—and changed its meaning and use forever. Caesar was just a family name until Julius came along: after that it became an official title, which, from that moment forward, would mean "the Emperor."[2] Julius Caesar's adopted nephew Octavian was given the title Augustus, which translates as "worthy of reverence." And both of their names were inserted vaingloriously into the Roman calendar—the one the world still uses today—throwing off the naming sequence for all time. Ever notice how *Sept*ember should be the 7th month, *Oct*ober the 8th, *Novem*ber the 9th, and *Decem*ber—as in *deca*—the 10th? That's because new months, the best months—July and August— were wedged into the center after the fact. People change the meaning of names, just as names change the behavior of people.

It would be easy to say that believers have behaved badly over the years and, as a result, given *Christian* a bad name. Easy but untrue. The word *Christian* started out as a bad name. It was created as a smear, and for most of the first hundred years was used as a pejorative.[3] The term appears only three times in all of Scripture, the first in Acts 11:26: "…So it was that for an entire year they met with the church and taught a great many people, and it was in Antioch that the disciples were first called "*Christians*."[4] Some translations include the quotation marks, others do not. Either way, the spirit of how the label is applied is essentially the same as the way we use "air quotes" today—full of snark and contempt.

Let's keep in mind that *our* Jesus was not the only Jesus in town.[5] From the Greek form of the Jewish name Joshua—or savior—it was actually a common name. So early on a distinguishing label for the new believers was needed. One such label was the *Nazarenes* because Jesus came from Nazareth. Lest you think that this was a more neutral name, let's review the context in which it was used. "For we have found this man a plague, one who stirs up riots among all the Jews throughout the world and is a ringleader of the sect of the Nazarenes" (Acts 24:5). See. The world has been annoyed with Christians from Day 1.

The origin of the word *Christian* is easy to trace: it is simply a short form of the Greek *Christianos,* which means, literally, "one who belongs to or follows Christ." But the word we know as *Christ* today, the word that most Sunday School kids could tell you means "the anointed one," actually came into being from a seemingly random morphing of two pre-existing, utterly secular references. One was *Chrestos,* which meant "good" or "kind."[6] The Greeks used it to describe the early followers of Jesus in the same way we might use "goodie two-shoes" today. But why? What was it about these "Christians" that caused people to think they were so good? Hard to say for sure but we do know this: they were the first people in the ancient world to show full respect and inclusion to women, foreigners, and slaves, to practice the adoption of unwanted babies (infanticide by exposure was commonly practiced), to reject earthly wealth and pool their resources for the good of the community, and to "walk the walk" so strongly when it came to their beliefs that they were willing to suffer imprisonment or death rather than deny the truth of Jesus.[7] More than an abstract belief, or a make-a-quick-offering-and-get-back-to-the-party-faith, this was a way of life, the following of Jesus's lifestyle and teachings.

The new Christians themselves would not have called their behavior good, but rather, Spirit-led and obedient. They knew that Jesus himself had rejected the label—"Why do you call me good? No one is good except God alone" (Luke 18:19)—and, apparently, did not appreciate the sarcastic name. Some Greeks actually called them *Chrestians* instead of Christians.

The second linguistic tie-in is, again, intended as a putdown. The Greek word *chriein*, which is the etymological root of *christos*, means "to rub lightly or spread (some substance, e.g. oil or liquid) over." *Chriein* has no sacred connotations as in "anointing," but indicates a person or object smeared with whitewash, cosmetics, paint—even, in the case of its use in the works of Homer, poison.[8] When it is applied towards a person, it connotes dishonor or disrespect. This was the way *christos* was swirling in the air of the Greco-Roman world in the first few decades after Jesus's death and resurrection.

And then something truly inspired happened. The apostles took the worldly slights of the nickname "Christos" and claimed them for the narrative of God.

"The beginning of the good news of **Jesus Christ...**" (Mark 1:1).

Let's look carefully at what was accomplished in the pairing of these two words. The earthly name of Jesus already represents the full promises of the Hebrew covenant (*yosha'* = *savior*). Now, the logical, consistent, obvious thing to do if they wanted to claim that the promises of the Old Testament had been fulfilled in Jesus would have been to use the Hebrew word *Messiah ("anointed")*. Or even the Greek word *eleimmenos,* which already existed and which conveyed the specific, sacred meaning, "anointed."[9]   But no. Mark, Matthew, Luke and Paul each own the outsider language of *Christos*, and, in effect, gave the culture in which Jesus lived an equal say in the naming of God. **Jesus**, from the ancient Hebrew; **Christ**, right out of the banter of the 1st century chat rooms. A **name** for the Word of God that is at once timeless and timely.

Peter urges the early believers to wear the moniker proudly. "Yet if anyone suffers as a Christian, let him not be ashamed, but let him glorify God in that name" (1 Peter 4:16). And, as the Scriptures come to a close, John makes clear with the least ambiguity that the

Messiah and the Christ are one and the same proclamation.[10]

Which brings us to the true matter at hand: not the name Christian—which is and always will be easy to mock—but the name *Jesus*. **Jesus**, the Son of God. **Jesus**, the Word of God. **Jesus**, "the image of the invisible God." *Jesus* as God's earthly, walking around, real-time, flesh and blood name—a name that was meant to be spoken, breaking the mold of reverence that still leads the Jewish faithful today to write G-D. Jesus is, like all human names, the part of a person that exists for the purpose of creating relationships. It is an invitation. An opening. God with a nametag on at the company mixer: HELLO, my name is….

Scary. Truly. The name **Jesus** is simply too powerful for words. Because beneath the wing of its five little letters is hidden the whole of God's love, mercy, grace, power, healing, forgiveness, redemption, and divine call. Certainly this is what we see in the book of Acts, which records all the miracles of Christ's ministry *after* he had been crucified and raised. Beginning with Pentecost and Peter's explanation of how each apostle was suddenly able to speak in languages any and all could understand, the **name of Jesus**, the risen Lord, begins to be revealed as **the word above all words**:

> In the last days it shall be, God declares,
> that I will pour out my Spirit on all flesh,

and your sons and your daughters
shall prophesy,
and your young men shall see visions,
and your old men shall dream dreams.
even on my male servants and
female servants,
in those days I will pour out my Spirit;
and they shall prophesy.
And I will show wonders in the
heavens above
and signs on the earth below,
blood, and fire, and vapor of smoke;
the sun shall be turned to darkness
and the moon to blood,
before the day of the Lord comes, the
great and magnificent day.
And it shall come to pass that everyone
who calls upon the name of the Lord shall
be saved (Acts 2:17- 21).

Soon thereafter Peter cuts the crowd of Israelites "to the heart" and calls them to "Repent and be baptized every one of you in **the name of Jesus Christ**" (Acts 2:38). As the apostles' ministry continued, they began to understand that the power that was given them in the Holy Spirit was present and transferable in **Jesus's name**.

Now Peter and John were going up to
the temple at the hour of prayer, the
ninth hour. And a man lame from birth

was being carried, whom they laid daily
at the gate of the temple that is called the
Beautiful Gate to ask alms of those
entering the temple. Seeing Peter and
John about to go into the temple, he
asked to receive alms. And Peter
directed his gaze at him, as did John, and
said, "Look at us." And he fixed his
attention on them, expecting to receive
something from them. But Peter said, "I
have no silver and gold, but what I do
have I give to you. In the name of Jesus
Christ of Nazareth, rise up and walk!"
And he took him by the right hand and
raised him up, and immediately his feet
and ankles were made strong (Acts 3:1-
7).

The people gathered at Solomon's Portico were "utterly
astonished." Peter attempts to explain the ineffable: that
they had killed Jesus, "the Author of life," but the God of
Abraham, Isaac, and Jacob has raised and glorified
Him—and **his name**.

And **his name—by faith in his name—**
has made this man strong whom you see
and know, and the faith that is through
Jesus has given the man this perfect
health in the presence of you all (Acts
3:16).

Peter and John continued to preach, threatening the status quo and prompting their arrest. Still, what the people had heard in the name of Jesus was already rooted in their hearts, "...many of those who heard **the word** believed, and the number of the men came to about five thousand" (Acts 4:4). On trial to defend the source of their power, Peter

> filled with the Holy Spirit, said to them, "Rulers of the people and elders, if we are being examined today concerning a good deed done to a crippled man, by what means this man has been healed, let it be known to all of you and to all the people of Israel that by **the name of Jesus Christ of Nazareth**, whom you crucified, whom God raised from the dead—by him this man is standing before you well. This Jesus is the stone that was rejected by you, the builders, which has become the cornerstone. And there is salvation in no one else, for there is no other name under heaven given among men **by which we must be saved**" (Acts 4:8-12).

Unnerved by the apostles' boldness, and unable to put the miracles back in the box, the council endeavored to keep **the word** from spreading: "So they called them and charged them not to speak or teach at all **in the name of**

Jesus" (Acts 4:18). The apostles refused to comply, gathering with their fellow believers for prayer.

> And now, Lord, look at their threats, and grant to your servants to continue to speak **your word** with all boldness, while you stretch out your hand to heal, and signs and wonders are performed **through the name of your holy servant Jesus**. And when they had prayed, the place in which they were gathered together was shaken, and they were all filled with the Holy Spirit and continued to speak **the word of God** with boldness (Acts 4:29-31).

What's in a name, we ask? When the name is **Jesus**, the whole of the universe, the boldness to speak its truth, and the ability to be changed forever upon its hearing. Even the authorities were convinced that time would reveal the truth of the **name of Jesus**, as a council member named Gamaliel used logic and empirical evidence to persuade them: "if this plan or this undertaking is of man, it will fail; but if it is of God—you will not be able to overthrow them" (Acts 5:38-39). And so the apostles were ordered once again not to speak **in the name of Jesus** and, once again, they ignored the order, proceeding to teach and preach in **His name** in the temple and at home and in the street and to the ends of the earth. Asia. Africa. India. Europe. Consider these historical facts from Phillip Jenkins' sweeping work, *The Next Christendom*:

- Despite the common perception in the Western world, Christianity was, for the first thousand years, actually much stronger in Asia and North Africa than in Europe. Much of what we call the Muslim world today was once the heartland of Christianity.

- During the first two centuries of the Christian era, Syria, Egypt and Mesopotamia (modern Iraq) became the centers of Christian life, giving birth to the first Christian art, literature, and music. Some of the best-known Arab writers, including Khalil Gibran, author of *The Prophet*, were and are, Christian.

- The Gospels and the Psalms were already available in Coptic by around 300 AD. While other North African nations adopted the Latin language of the Church—and were overtaken by Muslim conquerors— the Coptic Christians in Egypt kept their "native tongue" and never lost their faith: Still today there are over 10 million Coptic Christians in Egypt.

- In the early 4th century, it was Armenia—not Rome—that first declared

Christianity as its official religion, with Ethiopia fast on its heels.

- By the time Anglo-Saxons were converted in England, Ethiopian Christianity was already in its tenth generation.
- Missionaries from the Church of the East (deemed heretical by the church in Rome), made inroads to China along the Silk Route, leading, in 638, to the building of the first church in China's capital of Ch'ang'an. Just as Paul tried to "translate" the Gospel using concepts and images that the Greco-Roman world would understand, the Church of the East was interacting closely with other world religions; in both India and China, we find an ancient symbol combining the Christian cross with the Buddhist lotus.
- In 2010, there were 544 million Christians in Latin America, 286 million in North America, 352 million in Asia, and 493 million in Africa.
- By 2050 only about 1/5 of the world's 3.2 billion Christians will be non-Hispanic whites, and the idea of a "white Christian" will be as quirky as, say, a "Swedish Buddhist."[11]

Why do these facts matter? Because they upend a gross misperception that many have about what a *Christian* is—what we look like, where we come from. In the Western world, many outside the church think of Christianity as a religion of "white people," with a conciliatory nod to the black churches and the Hispanic Catholics. As each generation becomes more and more globally and multi-culturally aware and engaged, this seemingly "old-fashioned" religion is just not considered hip or cool or relevant enough. Aging Boomers and Gen-Xers and Millennials want to dabble in more exotic flavors, with ties to the "hipper, sexier, more mystical," countries like Africa, India, Asia, and Latin America. They want the religions of *dim sum* and *tapas* and *samosas*, tasty little bites of global culture, and music with a primitive new beat. Well, if the benchmark for a good religion is what's trending on Twitter, watch out. Because not only is Christianity the most global religion on the planet *historically*, it is the most multi-ethnic, multi-cultural religion on earth today and will be for as far into the future as our greatest data-driven minds can project.

Just as the wise Pharisee Gamaliel had observed two thousand years ago: if those who preach in **the name of Jesus** are of God, "you will not be able to overthrow them."[12] It was this same Gamaliel who had been the chief teacher and mentor of Paul back when he was still a good Jew named Saul. And it was Paul who would give his life to help establish the early churches that would make good on Jesus's final words before His visible Ascension, that they would be His witnesses "to the ends of the earth."[13]

The divine plan for **the Word of God** will be carried out with or without us. But when we wear the mantle of *Christian* as if it were a cape or a crown, we create stumbling blocks for people who desperately long for the peace "which surpasses all understanding" (Philippians 4:7). More than the misunderstanding of all the loaded bible words discussed in this book, more than the misperception of Christianity as an old, dying, white person's religion, more even than the constant persecution from the camps of science and atheism and the culture, it is the **words of Christians** themselves that do the most harm to the cause of the Gospel. It is because of this that we are instructed to "be quick to hear, slow to speak, slow to anger; for the anger of man does not produce the righteousness of God" (James 1:19).

> For every kind of beast and bird, of reptile and sea creature, can be tamed and has been tamed by mankind, but no human being can tame the tongue. It is a restless evil, full of deadly poison. With it we bless our Lord and Father, and with it we curse people who are made in the likeness of God. From the same mouth come blessing and cursing. My brothers,

these things ought not to be so (James 3:7-10).

And so as James, the brother of Jesus, tells us, we are to choose our words not only wisely, but sparingly, as if our voices had no other use than praising the Lord, or helping a neighbor to find his way back to Him.

Today, as we make our way through the 21st century, we will be ushering in an explosive era of the new colors and voices and sounds of Jesus alive and at work in the world. A missionary is no longer a white person travelling to the majority world, but rather, missionaries are being sent from China to the Middle East, from Kenya to Europe, as the vibrant faithful seek to enrich and rekindle the souls of those regions that have cast off the Word of God with a cynical shrug.

So much change can be uncomfortable for some, but God tells us to "Fear not!" Let us come alongside the unfamiliar faces and tongues and songs. Let us celebrate the mystery of that five-letter word, **Jesus**, unpacking "all the words of this Life" (Acts 5:20) in a language each people can understand. Let us celebrate the fact that our faith is the most multi-cultural body of believers in all of human history. Let us seek Him with all our hearts, souls and minds, and when we hear His voice, let us honor it by being "impeccable" with His Word.

For some contemporary believers, the name *Christian* has become so heavy-laden with social, political and doctrinal baggage that they have cast it off, opting instead to call themselves Jesus Followers, or Followers of The Way. "The Way," was one of first terms the first Christians used to describe their new life in Jesus Christ. It was the only descriptor that was used by insiders and outsiders alike. Saul travelled the Damascus road to arrest anyone who belonged to "the Way" (Acts 9:2). Luke, Peter, and Paul all used "the Way" as their point of reference for the new way of life being lived in Jesus, who tells us that he is "the way, the truth and the life." The Way just might help us shake off the dust of two thousand years of baggage riding on the word *Christian*. Consider it a rebrand. Launch the ebook: *The Way: Ancient Truth for this Life and the Next*. Watch it shoot up the *NY Times* Bestseller's List, and people go all "starry-eyed" over this *new* teaching. This is the gift of Pentecost, that we may—we must—translate the Gospel into a language that people—even "spiritual but not religious" contemporary America—can understand.

May we do this boldly, trusting that the Word of God is the Word of God is the Word of God and by any other name, in any other language, in every era, despite all our failed attempts to express it, and all the muck the world hurls its way, will forever "smell as sweet." People, cultures, and beliefs will come and go. But **Jesus Christ** is the same "yesterday and today and forever" (Hebrews 13:8).

Consider what you've read here. Consider what you've heard. Go out in the world with full confidence that, "Heaven and earth will pass away, but my words will not pass away" (Mark 13:31). While we're here, may we use them well.

CHRISTIAN
UNLOADED

- A Christian is, literally, "one who belongs to Christ."

- The word "Christ" was appropriated from secular words.

- Christian is not a title but a way of life.

- "A Christian is a perfectly free lord of all, subject to none. A Christian is a perfectly dutiful servant of all, subject *of* all, subject *to* all." — Martin Luther

Study Questions
CHRISTIAN

1. What are some of the negative images that come to mind when you consider what the culture thinks of *Christians*?

2. On page 180 we read the word Christian started out as a_____.

3. On pages 181-182 we learn the word Christ came from the morphing of two other first-century cultural words.

   Chrestos, which meant what? How did Jesus followers exhibit behavior like this?

   Chriein, which meant what? How is this different from the way we translate Christ?

4. After reading from pages 183, in your opinion what was accomplished when the early followers decided to own the slur *Christos* (rather than using either of the existing sacred words - *messiah* or *eleimmenos*)?

5. READ Acts 4:12. What are some of the ways this chapter explains the power in the Name of Jesus? Is this a new understanding for you, that there is power in his name alone?

6. On pages 189-190, the authors quote Philip
   Jenkins who provides a sweeping picture of
   global Christianity. Are these images different
   than the ones you usually consider when you hear
   the word Christian? Do you think the culture
   recognizes Christianity as being as multi-cultural
   as it is? Do you think it would matter to them if
   they did?

7. READ James 1:19-21 and 3:7-12. On page 192
   the authors state about words, it is the _____
   of _____ themselves that do the
   _____ to the cause of the Gospel. And on
   page 193, we are to choose our words
   _____, but _____, as
   if our voices had no other use than
   _____, or _____
   to find his way _____. What
   are your thoughts about these insights?

ABOUT THE AUTHORS

Heather Choate Davis began her career as an advertising copywriter and creative director working with Fortune 500 companies. She is an author, teacher, retreat leader, community organizer, and creator of The Renaissance Service™. She lives in Mar Vista, CA and is currently involved in revealing Christ through the ministry of LINC L.A. Her blog is at heatherchoatedavis.com, and you can follow her on Twitter @faithinwords.

Leann Luchinger built her first career in sales, marketing, and corporate communications, including a decade as Director of Communications for a global manufacturer. She is deeply involved with fundraising and communications leadership for several Orange County non-profits, as well as Concordia University and the LCMS. A skilled bible study "doctor" and teacher, she blogs at Leannderings.com. Follow her on Twitter @icktank.

Find out more about their work together at icktank.com.

BIBLIOGRAPHY

Alexander, Ralph H. "847 הדה,". In *Theological Wordbook of the Old Testament*, edited by R. Laird Harris, Gleason L. Archer Jr., & Bruce K. Waltke, 364. Chicago, IL: Moody Press, 1999.

Alexander, T. Desmond, and Brian S. Rosner, . *New Dictionary of Biblical Theology.* Downers Grove, IL: InterVarsity Press, 2000.

Alighieri, Dante. *Dante's Inferno.* Benton, AR: Benton Publishing Group, 2013.

Augustine. *The Confession.* Translated by Maria Boulding O.S.B. New York: Vintage Spiritual Classics, 1997.

Baille, Robert. *A Disuassive from the Errours of the Time.* 1645.

BandenBos, Gary R. *APA Dictionary of Psychology (1st edition).* Washington D.C.: American Psychological Association, 2007.

Barna Group. *Works Righteousness Among Lutherans.* Survey, Ventura, CA: Barna Group, 1997.

Bietenhard, H. "Ἅδης,". In *New International Dictionary of New Testament Theology*, edited by Lothar Coenen, Erich Bevreuther, & Hans Bietenhard, 206. Grand Rapids, MI: Zondervan Publishing House, 1986.

Bietenhard, H. "Hell, Abyss, Hades, Gehenna, Lower Regions." In *New Dictionary of New Testament Theology*, edited by Lothar Coenen, Erich Beyreuther, & Hans Bietenhard, 205. Grand Rapids, MI: Zondervan Publishing House, 1986.

Bietenhard, H., and C. Brown. "Satan, Beelzebul, Devil, Exorcism." In *New International Dictionary of*

New Testament Theology, edited by Lothar Coenen, Erich Beyreuther, & Hans Bietenhard, 468. Grand Rapids, MI: Zondervan Publishing House, 1986.

Bohn, Roger E., and James E. Short. *How Much Information?* Report on American Consumers, San Diego: University of California San Diego, 2009.

Bowling, Andrew. "907 יָדָא," In *Theological Wordbook of the Old Testament*, edited by Harris, Laird Archer Jr., Gleason L., & Bruce K. Waltke, 399. Chicago, IL: Moody Press, 1999.

Brown, C. and J. Schneider. "Σώζω" In *New International Dictionary of New Testament Theology*, edited by Lothar Coenen, Erich Beyreuther, & Hans Bietenhard, 208. Grand Rapids, MI: Zondervan Publishing House, 1986.

Brown, Colin. *New International Dictionary of New Testament Theology.* Grand Rapids, MI: Zondervan Publishing House, 1986.

Cairns, Scott. *Endless Life, Poems of the Mystics.* Brewster, MA: Paraclete Press, 2007.

Capes, David B., Rodney Reeves, and E. Randolph Richards. *Rediscovering Paul: An Introduction to His World, Letters and Theology.* Downers Grove, IL: InterVarsity Press, 2007.

Carpenter, Eugene E., and Philip W. Comfort. *Holmn Treasury of Key Bible words: 200 Greek and 200 Hebrew Words Defined and Explained.* Nashville, TN: Broadman & Holman Publishers, 2000.

Coenen, L. ""Church, Synagogue"." In *New International Dictionary of New Testament Theology*, edited by Lothar Coenen, Erich Beyreuther, & Hans Bietenhard, 292. Grand Rapids, MI: Zondervan Publishing House, 1986.

Coogan, Michael D., ed. *The New Oxford Annotated Bible, Third Edition. NRSV.* Oxford University Press, n.d.

Davis, Heather Choate. *From Sin to Death: The Inspired Logic of St. Paul.* Paper, Irvine: Concordia University, Irvine, 2012.

Davis, Heather Choate. *Reclaiming the Wisdom of "Homo Incurvatus In Se" Man Turned in on Himself as an Entry Point for the Discussion of Sin in 21st Century America.* Master's Thesis, Irvine: Concordia University, Irvine, 2013.

Eckman. "Cultural Dysfunction in21st-Century America." *Issues in Perspective.* August 23, 2014. http://graceuniversity.edu/iip/2014/08/cultural-dysfunction-in-21st-century-america/ (accessed 2014).

Efird, James M., and Mark Allan Powell. "Satan." In *The HarperCollins bible Dictionary (Revised and Updated)*, edited by Mark Allan Powell, 922. New York: Harper collins, 2011.

Elwell, Walter A., and Barry J. Beitzel. *Baker Encyclopedia of the Bible.* Grand Rapids, MI: Baker Book House, 1988.

Family Guy Quotes. n.d. http://www.familyguyquotes.com/characters/tom-tucker-quotes-2.html (accessed April 2014).

Fee, Gordon D., and Douglas Stuart. *How to Read the Bible for All its Worth.* Grand Rapids: Zondervan, 2003.

Fürst, D. ""Confess"." In *New International Dictionary of New Testament Theology*, edited by Lothar Coenen, Erich Beyreuther, & Hans Beitenhard, 344. Grand Rapids, MI: Zondervan Publishing House, 1999.

Gunther, W. "Sin." In *New International Dictionary of New Testament Theology*, edited by Lothar Coenen, Erich Beyreuther, & Hans Bietenhard, 573. Grand Rapids: Zondervan Publishing House, 1986.

Guttentag, M., and P.E. Secord. *Too Many Women? The sex ration question.* Beverly Hills, CA: Sage, 1983.

Hansen, Gary Neal. *John Wesley's Small Group Agenda.* 2014. http://garynealhansen.com/john-wesleys-small-group-agenda/ (accessed April 2014).

Harris, M.J. ""Tent, Tabernacle"." In *New International Dictionary of New Testament Theology*, edited by Lothar Coenen, Erich Beyreuther, & Hans Bietenhard, 811. Grand Rapids, MI: Zondervan Publishing House, 1986.

Harris, R. Laird, Gleason Archer Jr., and Bruce K. Waltke, . *Theological Wordbook of the Old Testament.* Chicago, IL: Moody Press, 1999.

Hartley, John E. "929 ישע," In *Theological Wordbook of the Old Testament*, edited by R. Laird, Archer Jr., Gleason Harris, & Bruce K. Waltke, 414. Chicago, IL.: Moody Press, 1999.

Hoyt, Sarah F. "The Etymology of Religion." *The Journal of the American Oriental Society, Vol. 32, No. 2* (Johns Hopkins University), 1912: 126-129.

Hunter, David G. *Reclaiming Biblical Morality: Sex and Salvation History in Augustine's Treatment of the Hebrew Saints.* In Dominico Eloquio: In Lordly Eloquence, n.d.

Job, J.B. ""Religion"." In *New Bible Dictionary*, edited by D.R.W. Wood et al., 1007. Leicester, England; Downers Grove, IL: InterVarsity Press, 1996.

Kallem, Jaweed. "Huffington Post Religion." *http://www.huffingtonpost.com.* n.d.

http://www.huffingtonpost.com/2014/05/25/mem
orial-day-2014-observations_n_5389556.html
(accessed May 25, 2014).

Kolb, Robert, Timothy J. Wengert, and Charles P. Arand.
*The Book of Concord: The Confessions of the
Evangelical Lutheran Church.* Minneapolis, MN:
Fortress Press, 2000.

Laubach, F. "Conversion, Penitence, Repentance,
Proselyte." In *New International Dictionary of
New Testametn Theology*, edited by Lothar
Coenen, Erich Beyreuther, & Hans Beitenhard,
354. Grand Rapids, MI: Zondervan Publishing
House, 1986.

Lenski, R.C.H. *The Interpretation of St. Luke's Gospel.*
Minneapolis, MN: Augsburg Publishing House,
1961.

—. *The Interpretation of St. Matthew's Gospel.*
Minneapolis, MN: Augsburg Publishing House,
1961.

Lewis, C.S. *Mere Christianity.* New York: Harper
Collins, 1952.

—. *Readings for Meditation and Reflection "The Lion
and the Stream".* Edited by Walter Hooper. San
Francisco, CA: Harper Collins, 1996.

Lindbeck, George A. *Nature of Doctrine.* Louisville, KY:
Westminster/John Knox Press, 1984.

Luchinger, Leann. *Women in Service to the Church: A
Comparative Analysis of Martin Luther's Writings
on 1 Timothy 2:8-15 and His Personal
Correspondences with Women.* Master's Thesis,
Irvine: Concordia University , 2014.

Magedanz, Stacy. *CliffsNotes on St. Augustine's
Confessions.* Los Angeles, September 15, 2014.

Marshall, I.H. ""Jesus Christ, Titles Of"." In *New Bible
Dictionary*, edited by D.R.W. Wood et al., 575.

Leicester, England; Downers Grove, IL: InterVarsity Press, 1996.

Mathews, K.A. "Genesis 11:27-50:26, vol. 1B." In *The New American Commentary*, 183-187. Nashville, TN: Broadman & Holman Publishers, 2005.

Merriam-Webster's Collegiate Dictionary. Springfield, MA: Merriam-Webster, Inc., 2003.

Mundle, W. ""Fear, Awe"." In *New International Dictionary of New Testament Theology*, edited by Lothar Coenen, Erich Beyreuther, & Hans Bietenhard, 623. Grand Rapids, MI: Zondervan Publishing House, 1986.

Myers, Allen C. *The Eerdmans Bible Dictionary.* Grand Rapids, MI: Eerdmans, 1987.

Newton, John. "Amazing Grace." 1779.

Olson, Roger E. *The Story of Christian Theology.* Downers Grove: InterVarsity Press, 1999.

Payne, J.B. ""Judges, Book Of"." In *New Bible Dictionary*, edited by D.R.W. Wood et al., 627. Downers Grove, IL: InterVarsity Press, 2000.

Plato. *Gorgias, Excerpt 1.* Translated by Benjamin Jowett. Project Guttenberg, 2008.

Purdom, Charles Benjamin. *The God-Man: The Life Journeys and Work of Meher Baba with an Interpretation of His Silence and Spiritual Teaching.* Crescent Beach, S.C.: Sheriar Press, Inc., 1971.

Putnam, Robert D. *Bowling Alone.* Simon & Schuster, 2001.

Ranke-Heinemann, Uta. *Eunochs for the Kingdom of Heaven.* Translated by Peter Heinegg. New York: Doubleday, 1991.

Rengstorf, K.H. ""Jesus Christ, Nazarene, Christian"." In *New International Dictionary of New Testament Theology*, edited by Lothar Coenen, Erich

Beyreuther, & Hans Bietenhard, 331. Grand
Rapids, MI: Zondervan Publishing House, 1986.

Rengstorf, K.H. "χριστιανός," In *New International
Dictionary of New Testament Theology*, edited by
Lothar Coenen, Erich Beyreuther, & Hans
Bietenhard, 343. Grand Rapids, MI: Zondervan
Publishing House, 1986.

Rengstorf, K.H. "χριστς," In *New International
Dictionary of New Testament Theology*, edited by
Lothar Coenen, Erich Beyreuther, & Hans
Bietenhard, 334-335. Grand Rapids, MI:
Zondervan Publishing House, 1986.

Robinson, Simon J. "Opening Up 1 Timothy." In
Opening Up Commentary, 44. Leominster: Day
One Publications, 2004.

Rogers Jr., Cleon L., and Cleon L. Robers III. *The New
Linguistic and Exegetical Key to the Greek New
Testament.* Grand Rapids: Zondervan Publishing
House, 1998.

Schattenmann, J. "Κοινωνία," In In *New International
Dictionary of New Testament Theology*, edited by
Lothar Coenen, Erich Beyreuther, & Hans
Bietenhard, 639-640. Grand Rapids, MI:
Zondervan Publishing House, 1986.

Schneider, W. ""Judgment, Judge, Deliver, Judgment
Seat"." In *New International Dictionary of New
Testament Theology*, edited by Lothar Coenen,
Erich Beyreuther, & Hans Bietenhard, 363. Grand
Rapids, MI: Zondervan Publishing House, 1986.

Shakespeare, William. *Romeo and Juliet.* 1597.

Stark, Rodney. "Reconstructing the Rise of Christianity:
The Role of Women." *Sociology of Religion, Vol.
56. No 3*, Autumn, 1995: 229-244.

Strong LL.D., S.T.D., James. *The Strongest Strong's
Exhaustive concordance of the Bible.* Edited by

John R. Kohlenberger III, & James A. Swanson.
     Grand Rapids, IL: Zondervan Publishing House,
     2001.

—. *The Strongest Strong's Exhaustive Concordance of
     the Bible.* Edited by John R. Kohlenberger III, &
     James A. Swanson. Grand Rapids: Zondervan,
     2001.

Sutherland, John. "How Language is Literally Losing its
     Meaning." *The Guardian.* 2014.
     http://www.theguardian.com/science/shortcuts/20
     13/aug/14/language-literally-losing-its-meaning
     (accessed May 2014).

Swanson, James. *Dictionary of Biblical Languages with
     Semantic Domains: Greek (New Testament).* Oak
     Harbor: Logos Research Systems, Inc., 1997.

Tennyson, Alfred Lord. *Poems.* Edited by Hallam Lord
     Tennyson, & Alfred Lord and annotated by
     Tennyson. London: Macmillan, 1908.

Thiselton, Anthony C. *First Corinthians: A Shorter
     Exegetical and Pastoral Commentary.* Grand
     Rapids: William B. Eerdmans Publishing
     Company, 2006.

Towner, Philip H. *The Letters to Timothy and Titus.*
     Grand Rapids: William B. Eerdmans Publishing
     Company, 2006.

Updike, John. "Packed Dirt, Churchgoing, A Dying Cat,
     A Traded Car." *New Yorker*, December 16, 1961.

Walls, A.F. ""Christian"." In *New Bible Dictionary*,
     edited by D.R.W. Wood et al., 184. Leicester,
     England; Downers Grove, IL: InterVarsity Press,
     1996.

Weber, Carl Philip. "602 חָגַג," In *Theological Wordbook
     of the Old Testament*, edited by R. Laird Harris,
     Gleason L. Archer Jr., & Bruce K. Waltke, 261.
     Chicago, IL: Moody Press, 1999.

Weisberger, Lauren. *The Devil Wears Prada.* USA: Broadway Books, 2003.

Wolters, Al. ""An Early Parallel of αὐθεντέω in 1 Tim. 2:12." ." *Journal of the Evangelical Theological Society, Vol 54, No. 4,* December 2011: 677.

Young, Jun, and David Kinnaman. *The Hyperlinked Life: Live with Wisdom in an Age of Information Overload.* Grand Rapids, MI: Zonderfan Publishing House, 2013.

Zoppelt, Andy. *The Word that Changed the World.* 2006. http://www.therealchurch.com/articles/the_word_t hat_changed_the_world.html (accessed April 2014).

END NOTES

Chapter 1

[1] Roger E. Bohn and James E. Short, How Much Information? 2009 Report on American Consumers, University of California, San Diego.

[2] John Sutherland. "How Language is Literally Losing its Meaning." *The Guardian*. 2014. http://www.theguardian.com/science/shortcuts/2013/aug/14/language -literally-losing-its-meaning (accessed May 2014).

[3]. Walter A. Elwell and Barry J. Beitzel, *Baker Encyclopedia of the Bible* (Grand Rapids, MI: Baker Book House, 1988), 2159–2160.

[4] Walter A. Elwell and Barry J. Beitzel, *Baker Encyclopedia of the Bible* (Grand Rapids, MI: Baker Book House, 1988), 2159–2160.

[5] Colin Brown, *New International Dictionary of New Testament Theology* (Grand Rapids, MI: Zondervan Publishing House, 1986), 54.

[6] Jun Young & David Kinnaman, *The Hyperlinked Life: Live with Wisdom in an Age of Information Overload*, (Grand Rapids, Zondervan), 2013, 23.

Chapter 2

[1] Heather Choate Davis, "Reclaiming the Wisdom of *Homo Incurvatus In Se*: 'Man Turned in on Himself' as an Entry Point for the Discussion of Sin in 21st Century America," 2013.

[2] W. Günther, "Sin," ed. Lothar Coenen, Erich Beyreuther, and Hans Bietenhard, *New International Dictionary of New Testament Theology* (Grand Rapids, MI: Zondervan Publishing House, 1986), 573.

T. Desmond Alexander and Brian S. Rosner, eds., *New Dictionary of Biblical Theology* (Downers Grove, IL: InterVarsity Press, 2000).

[3] Alexander, *New Dictionary of Biblical Theology* 2000.

[4] Although theories of original sin had been presented as early as the 2nd century, Augustine was the first theologian to posit that the "disordered state" of physical lust satisfied through climax was the

entry point of sin. Uta Ranke-Heinemann, *Eunochs for the Kingdom of Heaven*, trans. Peter Heinegg (New York, Doubleday, 1991), 76.

[5] David G. Hunter, "Reclaiming Biblical Morality: Sex and Salvation History in Augustine's Treatment of the Hebrew Saints," *In Dominico Eloquio*: In Lordly Eloquence, 329-333.

[6] Heather Choate Davis, "From Sin to Death: The Inspired Logic of St. Paul," (Concordia University, 2012).

[7] David B. Capes, Rodney Reeves and E. Randolph Richards, *Rediscovering Paul: An Introduction to His World, Letters and Theology* (Downers Grove, IL, InterVarsity Press, 2007), 25.

[8] Plato, Gorgias, Excerpt 1, translated by Benjamin Jowett (Project Guttenberg eBook, 2008), p. 14.

[9] Robert Kolb, Timothy J. Wengert, and Charles P. Arand, *The Book of Concord: The Confessions of the Evangelical Lutheran Church* (Minneapolis, MN: Fortress Press, 2000), 113.

[10] Kolb, *The Book of Concord,* 2000, 40.

[11] Davis, *Homo Incurvatus In Se*, p. 2.

[12] Davis, *Homo Incurvatus In Se*, p. 5.

[13] Jenson, 16, referencing Richard Chenevix Trench, *Exposition of the Sermon on the Mount* (London: Macmillan and Co., 3rd ed, 1869), 116.

[14] Davis, *Homo Incurvatus in Se*, p, 20.

Chapter 3

[1] R. C. H. Lenski, *The Interpretation of St. Luke's Gospel* (Minneapolis, MN: Augsburg Publishing House, 1961), 723.

[2] F. Laubach, "Conversion, Penitence, Repentance, Proselyte," ed. Lothar Coenen, Erich Beyreuther, and Hans Bietenhard, *New International Dictionary of New Testament Theology* (Grand Rapids, MI: Zondervan Publishing House, 1986), 354.

[3] Robert Kolb, Timothy J. Wengert, and Charles P. Arand, *The Book of Concord: The Confessions of the Evangelical Lutheran Church* (Minneapolis, MN: Fortress Press, 2000), 161.

[4] *Metanoeō* or *Metanoia* both common repentance words are part of a group of words that mean "to think differently or reconsider."

epistrephō has a wider meaning than *metanoeō*, for it always includes faith. Laubach, "Conversion, Penitence, Repentance, Proselyte," 1986, 355.

[5] VandenBos, Gary R. (2007). *APA dictionary of psychology* (1st edition ed.). Washington, DC: American Psychological Association.

[6] Purdom, Charles Benjamin. *The God-Man: The Life, Journeys and Work of Meher Baba with an Interpretation of His Silence and Spiritual Teaching* (Crescent Beach, S. C.: Sheriar Press, Inc., 1971), 238.

[7] C.S. Lewis, *Mere Christianity*, (New York, Harper Collins), 1952, 56.

Chapter 4

[1] Family Guy Quotes. http://www.familyguyquotes.com/characters/tom-tucker-quotes-2.html

[2] The New Oxford Annotated Bible, Third Edition, NRSV. Edited by Michael D. Coogan, Oxford University Press, commentary, p. 999.

[3] H. Bietendhard, Ἅδης," ed. Lothar Coenen, Erich Beyreuther, and Hans Bietenhard, *New International Dictionary of New Testament Theology* (Grand Rapids, MI: Zondervan Publishing House, 1986), 206.

[4] Bietenhard, "Ἅδης," 1986, 206.

[5] Ibid.

[6] "Abyss" appears in Lk 8:31; Ro 10:7; "the bottomless pit" or "pit" appears in Rev 9:1, 2, 11; 11:7; 17:8; 20:1, 3. Strong's Greek #12 James Strong LL.D., S.T.D., *The Strongest Strong's Exhaustive Concordance of the Bible.* Edited by John R. Kohlenberger III, & James A. Swanson. (Grand Rapids: Zondervan, 2001).

[7] Rev. 9:11

[8] Rev.11:7; 17:8

[9] H. Bietenhard, "Hell, Abyss, Hades, Gehenna, Lower Regions," ed. Lothar Coenen, Erich Beyreuther, and Hans Bietenhard, *New International Dictionary of New Testament Theology* (Grand Rapids, MI: Zondervan Publishing House, 1986), 205.

[10] Jas 3:6 is the only occurrence of *gehenna* not spoken by Jesus.

[11] Bietenhard, "Hell, Abyss, Hades, Gehenna, Lower Regions," 1986,

205.

[12] Strong's Greek #1067. James Swanson, *Dictionary of Biblical Languages with Semantic Domains: Greek (New Testament)* (Oak Harbor: Logos Research Systems, Inc., 1997). Walter A. Elwell and Barry J. Beitzel, *Baker Encyclopedia of the Bible* (Grand Rapids, MI: Baker Book House, 1988), 844.

[13] Interview in *Playboy* magazine (1976), while a candidate for President.

[14] Gordon D. Fee and Douglas Stuart, How to Read the Bible for All Its Worth. (Grand Rapids, Zondervan. 2003),152.

[15] Dante Alighieri, "Dante's Inferno," (Benton, AR: Benton Publishing Group, 2013) Based on "The Vision of hell" by Dange Alighieri, tr. Rev. H.F. Cary, M.A. (London: Cassell & Company, Ltd., 1892).

[16] Bietenhard, "Hell, Abyss, Hades, Gehenna, Lower Regions," 1986, 208.

[17] Dante Alighieri, "Dante's Inferno," (Benton, AR:Benton Publishing Group, 2013) Based on "The Vision of hell" by Dange Alighieri, tr. Rev. H.F. Cary, M.A. (London: Cassell & Company, Ltd., 1892).

[18] T. Desmond Alexander and Brian S. Rosner, eds., *New Dictionary of Biblical Theology* (Downers Grove, IL: InterVarsity Press, 2000).

Chapter 5

[1] Eugene E. Carpenter and Philip W. Comfort, *Holman Treasury of Key Bible Words: 200 Greek and 200 Hebrew Words Defined and Explained* (Nashville, TN: Broadman & Holman Publishers, 2000), 161.

H. Bietenhard and C. Brown, "Satan, Beelzebul, Devil, Exorcism," ed. Lothar Coenen, Erich Beyreuther, and Hans Bietenhard, *New International Dictionary of New Testament Theology* (Grand Rapids, MI: Zondervan Publishing House, 1986), 468.

[2] R. C. H. Lenski, *The Interpretation of St. Matthew's Gospel* (Minneapolis, MN: Augsburg Publishing House, 1961), 139.

[3] Bietenhard, "Satan, Beelzebul, Devil, Exorcism," 1986, 468.

[4] Allen C. Myers, *The Eerdmans Bible Dictionary* (Grand Rapids, MI: Eerdmans, 1987), 914.

[5] Bietenhard, "Satan, Beelzebul, Devil, Exorcism," 1986, 469.

[6] Ibid., 470.

[7] According to scholars James M. Efird and Mark Allan Powell, it is likely that in the Lord's Prayer the petition traditionally rendered "deliver us from evil" would be better translated (as in the NRSV), "rescue us from the evil one" (Matt. 6:13b). James M. Efird and Mark Allan Powell, "Satan," ed. Mark Allan Powell, *The HarperCollins Bible Dictionary (Revised and Updated)* (New York: HarperCollins, 2011), 922. Bietenhard, "Satan, Beelzebul, Devil, Exorcism," 1986, 470.

[8] Lenski, *The Interpretation of St. Matthew's Gospel* 1961, 142.

[9] Robert Kolb, Timothy J. Wengert, and Charles P. Arand, *The Book of Concord: The Confessions of the Evangelical Lutheran Church* (Minneapolis, MN: Fortress Press, 2000), 142.

[10] C.S. Lewis, Readings for Meditation and Reflection, edited by Walter Hooper, "The Lion and the Stream" (Harper Collins, San Francisco, 1996),1.

[11] Walter A. Elwell and Barry J. Beitzel, *Baker Encyclopedia of the Bible* (Grand Rapids, MI: Baker Book House, 1988), 1908.

[12] Bietenhard, "Satan, Beelzebul, Devil, Exorcism," 1986, 470.

Chapter 6

[1] T. Desmond Alexander and Brian S. Rosner, eds., *New Dictionary of Biblical Theology* (Downers Grove, IL: InterVarsity Press, 2000).

[2] Alexander, *New Dictionary of Biblical Theology*, 2000.

[3] The Barna Report, Ventura, CA: Barna Group, 1997, as cited in TEXN 520 Romans with an Introduction to Other Pauline Epistles, Dr. Michael Middendorf, 2012, Concordia University.

[4] John E. Hartley, "929 יָשַׁע," ed. R. Laird Harris, Gleason L. Archer Jr., and Bruce K. Waltke, *Theological Wordbook of the Old Testament* (Chicago: Moody Press, 1999), 414.

[5] Leann Luchinger. Gospel First: A study of the 10 Commandments.

[6] C. Brown and J. Schneider, ed. Lothar Coenen, Erich Beyreuther, and Hans Bietenhard, *New International Dictionary of New Testament Theology* (Grand Rapids, MI: Zondervan Publishing House, 1986), 208.

[7] Hermann Sasse, "Union and Confession [1936]," TLW 1, Kindle Location 6389.

[8] *Amazing Grace*. John Newton, 1779.

Chapter 7

[1] Ralph H. Alexander. "847 ידה ed. R. Laird Harris, Gleason L. Archer Jr., and Bruce K. Waltke, Theological Wordbook of the Old Testament (Chicago: Moody Press, 1999), 364.

[2] Alexander, "847 ידה," 1999, 365.

[3] Augustine, *The Confession,* Translated by Maria Boulding O.S.B.. New York, Vintage

   Spiritual Classics, 1997, p. 69.

[4] Magedanz, Stacy. *CliffsNotes on St. Augustine's Confessions.* 15 Sep 2014
</literature/s/st-augustines-confessions/book-summary>.

[5] Robert D. Putnam, *Bowling Alone.* Simon & Schuster, 2001.

[6] Jim Eckman, Issues in Perspective, "Cultural Dysfunction in 21st-Century America" Aug. 23, 2014, http://graceuniversity.edu/iip/2014/08/cultural-dysfunction-in-21st-century-america/

[7] R. Laird Harris, Gleason L. Archer Jr., and Bruce K. Waltke, eds., Theological Wordbook of the Old Testament (Chicago: Moody Press, 1999), 241.

[8] D, "Confess," ed. Lothar Coenen, Erich Beyreuther, and Hans Bietenhard, *New International Dictionary of New Testament Theology* (Grand Rapids, MI: Zondervan Publishing House, 1986), 344.

[9] *Merriam-Webster's Collegiate Dictionary.* (Springfield, MA: Merriam-Webster, Inc., 2003).

[10] Roger E. Olson, The Story of Christian Theology (Downers Grove: InterVarsity Press, 1999) 129-30.

[11] Catholic simply means "universal."

[12] Gary Neal Hansen, *John Wesley's Small Group Agenda.* 2014. http://garynealhansen.com/john-wesleys-small-group-agenda/ (accessed April 2014).

[13] Hansen, *John Wesley's Small Group Agenda.* 2014.

Chapter 8

[1] Alfred Lord Tennyson Memorializing Events in the Battle of Balaclava, October 25, 1854.

[2] "Maidservant" (*šipḥâ*) is not a common slave but the personal servant of the "mistress" (*gĕbîrâ/gĕberet*, vv. 4, 8–9) of the house (cf. Ps 123:2; Prov 30:23; Isa 24:2).

A. Jepsen, "Amah and Schipchah," *VT* 8 (1958): 293–97, referenced in Westermann, *Genesis 12–36*, 238.

[3] Abram, however, does not give her to Sarai to do whatever she pleases; rather, she is to treat Hagar as she sees "best" (*haṭṭôb*, "the good"). K. A. Mathews, *Genesis 11:27–50:26*, vol. 1B, The New American Commentary (Nashville: Broadman & Holman Publishers, 2005), 183–187.

[4] Gen 41:40 Strong's Hebrew #5401 – kiss; Gen 49:15 Strong's Hebrew #H1961 + #5647 – be, become + work, serve; Dt. 20:12 Strong's Hebrew #7999 (#2401c) – be in a covenant of peace; 2 Ch. 30:8 Strong's Hebrew #5414 + #3027- give + allegiance; Job 22:21 Strong's Hebrew #5532 – be of use, service; Ps 68:31 Strong's Hebrew #3027 – abandon, allegiance, alongside; Ps. 81;11 Strong's Hebrew #14 – be willing, consent; Pr. 3:6 Strong's Hebrew #3045 – know, knowledge; Lam. 5:6 Strong's Hebrew #5414 + #H3027 – give + abandon, allegiance.

[5] Leann Luchinger, Co-humanity, Partnership, and Leadership: Christianity and Women in Roman Antiquity. (Concordia University Irvine; 2012).

[6] Strong's Greek #5293 (5718) – be obedient, bring under control. The pres. Imp. tense points to the continual action or state of giving Himself. In a time when marriages were arranged and morals were loose, to fulfill the commands of subordination and love was not an easy task. For marriage and the home in the ancient world, including both Jewish and Gentile. Cleon L. Rogters Jr and Cleon L. Rogers III, The New Linguistic and Exegetical Key to the Greek New Testament. (Grand Rapids; Zondervan. 1998) 445.

[7] Rodney Stark, Reconstructing the Rise of Christianity: The Role of Women. *Sociology of Religion, Vol. 56. No 3*, Autumn, 1995: 229-244.

[8] Towner, The Letters of Timothy and Titus, 2006. Anthony C. Thiselton, 1 Corinthians: A Shorter Exegetical & Pastoral

Commentary, (Grand Rapids; Eerdmans. 2006).

[9] David B. Capes, Rodney Reeves, and E. Randolph Richards. *Rediscovering Paul:*

An Introduction to His World, Letters and Theology. (Downers Grove, IL: InterVarsity Press, 2007), 226-230.

[10] T. Desmond Alexander, Brian S. Rosner, D.A. Carson, and Graeme Goldsworthy, *New Dictionary of Biblical Theology.* (Downers Grove: InterVarsity Press, 2000) 331.

[11] Simon J. Robinson, *Opening up 1 Timothy*, Opening Up Commentary (Leominster: Day One Publications, 2004), 44.

[12] Philip H. Towner, *The Letters to Timothy and Titus.* (Grand Rapids: William B. Eerdmans Publishing Company, 2006) 48.

[13] Leann Luchinger, Women in Service to the Church: A Comparative Analysis of Martin Luther's Writings on 1 Timothy 2:8-15 and His Personal Correspondences with Women (Concordia University Irving, 2014).

[14] Al Wolters, "An Early Parallel of αὐθεντέω in 1 Tim. 2:12." *Journal of the Evangelical Theological Society* Vol. 54, No. 4 (December 2011) 677.

[15] 1 Corinthians 7:3

[16] Thiselton, 1 Corinthians, 2006. 101-103.

[17] Gordon D. Fee and Douglas Stuart, How to Read the Bible for All Its Worth. (Grand Rapids, Zondervan. 2003),74.

Chapter 9

[1] The tabernacle was, in effect, a portable tent for worship. M. J. Harris et al., "Tent, Tabernacle," ed. Lothar Coenen, Erich Beyreuther, and Hans Bietenhard, *New International Dictionary of New Testament Theology* (Grand Rapids, MI: Zondervan Publishing House, 1986), 811.

[2] 1 Kings 8:27, 2 Chron. 2:6

[3] Jeremiah 7, 1 Kings 8:27-30, Ezekial 10

[4] [Middle English *chirche*, from Old English *cirice*, ultimately from Late Greek *kyriakon*, from Greek, neuter of *kyriakos* of the lord, from *kyrios* lord, master; akin to Sanskrit *śūra* hero, warrior] before 12th century. Merriam-Webster,Inc. *Merriam-Webster's Collegiate Dictionary.* (Springfield, MA: Merriam-Webster, Inc., 2003).

[5] Andy Zoppelt. *The Word that Changed the World.* 2006. http://www.therealchurch.com/articles/the_word_that_changed_the_world.html

[6] Derived from *synagō*, bring together, and attested from the 5th cent. B.C. onwards. L. Coenen, "Church, Synagogue," ed. Lothar Coenen, Erich Beyreuther, and Hans Bietenhard, *New International Dictionary of New Testament Theology* (Grand Rapids, MI: Zondervan Publishing House, 1986), 292.

[7] It is attested from Eur. and Hdt. onwards (5th cent. B.C.), and denotes in the usage of antiquity the popular assembly of the competent full citizens of the polis, city. Coenen, "Church, Synagogue," 1986, 291.

[8] John Updike, "Packed Dirt, Churchgoing, A Dying Cat, A Traded Car." *New Yorker*, December 16, 1961.

Regarding Noumenal: Scott Cairns, *Endless Life, Poems of the Mystics.* Brewster, MA: Paraclete Press, 2007.

[9] Mt. 16:18 and 18:17. T. Desmond Alexander and Brian S. Rosner, eds., *New Dictionary of Biblical Theology* (Downers Grove, IL: InterVarsity Press, 2000). 409-410.

[10] Robert D. Putnam, *Bowling Alone.* Simon & Schuster, 2001.

[11] J. Schattenmann, Κοινωνία," ed. Lothar Coenen, Erich Beyreuther, and Hans Bietenhard, *New International Dictionary of New Testament Theology* (Grand Rapids, MI: Zondervan Publishing House, 1986), 639–640. Eugene E. Carpenter and Philip W. Comfort, *Holman Treasury of Key Bible Words: 200 Greek and 200 Hebrew Words Defined and Explained* (Nashville, TN: Broadman & Holman Publishers, 2000), 280. Walter A. Elwell and Barry J. Beitzel, *Baker Encyclopedia of the Bible* (Grand Rapids, MI: Baker Book House, 1988), 789.

[12] From the Hebrew (edah). Coenen, "Church, Synagogue," 1986, 294.

[13] Robert Kolb, Timothy J. Wengert, and Charles P. Arand, *The Book of Concord: The Confessions of the Evangelical Lutheran Church* (Minneapolis, MN: Fortress Press, 2000), 382.

[14] Kolb, *The Book of Concord*, 2000, 383.

[15] Elwell, *Baker Encyclopedia of the Bible*, 1988, 459.

Chapter 10

[1] "I Have a Dream" was a public speech delivered on August 28, 1963 by American civil rights activist Martin Luther King, Jr. calling for an end to racism in the U.S.

[2] W. Schneider, "Judgment, Judge, Deliver, Judgment Seat," ed. Lothar Coenen, Erich Beyreuther, and Hans Bietenhard, *New International Dictionary of New Testament Theology* (Grand Rapids, MI: Zondervan Publishing House, 1986), 363.

[3] T. Desmond Alexander and Brian S. Rosner, eds., *New Dictionary of Biblical Theology* (Downers Grove, IL: InterVarsity Press, 2000).

[4] J. B. Payne, "Judges, Book Of," ed. D. R. W. Wood et al., *New Bible Dictionary* (Leicester, England; Downers Grove, IL: InterVarsity Press, 1996), 627.

[5] Schneider, "Judgment, Judge, Deliver, Judgment Seat," 1986, 362.

[6] John 7:24

[7] John 7:23

[8] The New Oxford Annotated Bible, Third Edition, NRSV. Edited by Michael D. Coogan, Oxford University Press, commentary, p. 354.

Chapter 11

[1] Paul James and Peter Mandaville (2010). *Globalization and Culture, Vol. 2: Globalizing Religions.* London:Sage Publications.

[2] J. B. Job, "Religion," ed. D. R. W. Wood et al., *New Bible Dictionary* (Leicester, England; Downers Grove, IL: InterVarsity Press, 1996), 1007.

[3] Sarah F. Hoyt, "The Etymology of Religion." *The Journal of the American Oriental Society, Vol. 32, No. 2* (Johns Hopkins University), 1912: 126-129.

[4] Hoyt, "The Etymology of Religion." 1912, 126-129.

[5] George A. Lindbeck, *Nature of Doctrine* (Louisville: Westminster/John Knox Press, 1984), 33.

[6] Carl Philip Weber, "602 גאה," ed. R. Laird Harris, Gleason L. Archer Jr., and Bruce K. Waltke, *Theological Wordbook of the Old Testament* (Chicago: Moody Press, 1999), 261.

[7] Huffington Post: Religion, Jaweed Kallem, May 25, 2014
http://www.huffingtonpost.com/2014/05/25/memorial-day-2014-observations_n_5389556.html

[8] Weber, "602 הגה," 1999, 261–262.

[9] Robert Baillie, A *Disuassive from the Errours of the Time (1645)*

[10] Andrew Bowlinged. R. Laird Harris, Gleason L. Archer Jr., and Bruce K. Waltke, *Theological Wordbook of the Old Testament* (Chicago: Moody Press, 1999), 399. W. Mundle, "Fear, Awe," ed. Lothar Coenen, Erich Beyreuther, and Hans Bietenhard, *New International Dictionary of New Testament Theology* (Grand Rapids, MI: Zondervan Publishing House, 1986), 623.

[11] Job, "Religion," 1996, 1007.

Chapter 12

[1] William Shakespeare, Romeo and Juliet. 1597.

[2] I. H. Marshall, "Jesus Christ, Titles Of," ed. D. R. W. Wood et al., *New Bible Dictionary* (Leicester, England; Downers Grove, IL: InterVarsity Press, 1996), 575.

[3] K.H. Rengstorf, "Χριστιανός," ed. Lothar Coenen, Erich Beyreuther, and Hans Bietenhard, *New International Dictionary of New Testament Theology* (Grand Rapids, MI: Zondervan Publishing House, 1986), 343.

[4] New Revised Standard Version

[5] K. H. Rengstorf, "Jesus Christ, Nazarene, Christian," ed. Lothar Coenen, Erich Beyreuther, and Hans Bietenhard, *New International Dictionary of New Testament Theology* (Grand Rapids, MI: Zondervan Publishing House, 1986), 331.

[6] Eugene E. Carpenter and Philip W. Comfort, *Holman Treasury of Key Bible Words: 200 Greek and 200 Hebrew Words Defined and Explained* (Nashville, TN: Broadman & Holman Publishers, 2000), 251. A. F. Walls, "Christian," ed. D. R. W. Wood et al., *New Bible Dictionary* (Leicester, England; Downers Grove, IL: InterVarsity Press, 1996), 184.

[7] Rodney Stark, "Reconstructing the Rise of Christianity: The Role of Women." (*Sociology of Religion*: Oxford University Press, Vol. 56, No. 3 Autumn 1995) 234-235. Guttentag, M., and P. E. Secord. 1983.Too many women? The sex ratio question. Beverly Hills, CA: Sage.

[8] Rengstorf, "Χρισός," 1986, 334-335.

[9] *Eleimmenos*, see Matthew 6:17.

[10] See John 1:41 and John 4:25. Rengstorf, "Χρισός," 1986, 338.

[11] Philip Jenkins, The New Christendom: the Coming of Global Christianity. (Oxford: Oxford University Press. 2011) pp.3, 21, 23, 25, 29, 32-33.

[12] Acts 5:39

[13] Acts 13:47

19791670R00136

Made in the USA
Middletown, DE
04 May 2015